DOVE OF GOLD

Dove of Gold

AND OTHER SIGNPOSTS OF THE SPIRIT

By LESLIE HARDINGE

TEACH Services, Inc.
Brushton, New York

PRINTED IN
THE UNITED STATES OF AMERICA

World rights reserved. This book or any portion thereof may not be copied or reproduced in any form or manner whatever, except as provided by law, without the written permission of the publisher, except by a reviewer who may quote brief passages in a review.

The author assumes full responsibility for the accuracy
of all facts and quotations as cited in this book.

Facsimile Reproduction

As this book played a formative role in the development of Christian thought and the publisher feels that this book, with its candor and depth, still holds significance for the church today. Therefore the publisher has chosen to reproduce this historical classic from an original copy. Frequent variations in the quality of the print are unavoidable due to the condition of the original. Thus the print may look darker or lighter or appear to be missing detail, more in some places than in others.

2006 07 08 09 10 11 12 · 5 4 3 2 1

Copyright © 2006 TEACH Services, Inc.
ISBN-13: 978-1-57258-058-9
ISBN 1-57258-058-5
Library of Congress Control Number: 95-61784

Published by

TEACH Services, Inc.
www.TEACHServices.com

CONTENTS

Prologue		7
1/Dove of Gold—Ambassador of God		9
2/Manna—Fare of God		17
3/Salt—Preserving of God		26
4/Seal—Signet of God		32
5/Earnest—Dowry of God		42
6/Oil—Luminance of God		53
7/Ointment—Authority of God		61
8/Rain—Nourisher of God		72
9/Dew—Nurture of God		86
10/Wind—Power of God		97
11/Light—Radiance of God		107
12/Fire—Cleansing of God		117
13/Hand—Fellowship of God		131
14/Breath—Life of God		142
15/Finger—Guidance of God		155
16/Eye—Discernment of God		163
17/Voice—Remembrancer of God		172
18/Sap—Life Current of God		182
Epilogue		191

PROLOGUE

There are many ways of studying the Scriptures. Each method has its merits, each its rewards. One of the more difficult Biblical topics is a consideration of the Holy Spirit. *Dove of Gold* assumes the personality of the Third Person of the heavenly Trio and bases many of its conclusions on the Deity of this Representative of the Lord Jesus Christ.

It approaches the vast subject of the Holy Spirit by viewing His functions through illustrations He Himself has selected as vehicles for the revelation of His character and work. In both the Old and the New Testaments several carefully chosen and highly suggestive symbols picture His activities. They have to do with natural objects, and through them the mind can easily pass from the known to the lesser known. Imagine each symbol to be a many-faceted gem. Lift it up, and allow the light of the Sun of Righteousness to fall upon it. Turn it around; and observe the flashing of light from each facet. Such study requires leisure and careful thought. As one observes the related aspects of the nature and function of the natural object used as a symbol, the work of the Holy Spirit will become clearer, and His disposition of concern and affection much more appealing. The eighteen symbols we shall study cover every aspect of His ministry.

We should pray, as we enter upon this study of the most mighty Agency at work in the world today, "Eternal Spirit, enlighten us with Thy light and lead us to Him who is the Light of the world, whose Representative Thou art. Amen."

1.

DOVE OF GOLD --
Ambassador of God

Jesus deliberately turned His back on the carpenter's shop at Nazareth. Mingling with the crowds gathered about the Baptist on the banks of the Jordan, He presented Himself for baptism to seal His severance from His past life. "Comest thou to me?" the Baptizer tried to dissuade Him. "Suffer it to be so now," Christ gently replied. Then the two men waded into the muddy stream, and John baptized the Son of God. The peace and seclusion of His life at Nazareth had passed and were buried in Jordan's flood. Now Christ awaited trial and conflict and death.

Climbing back to the bank, Jesus knelt in supplication to His Father. "Never before have the angels listened to such a prayer." —Ellen G. White, *The Desire of Ages*, p. 112. Christ begged for the assurance of God's presence and asked for strength to carry out the most difficult task ever attempted. Unseen beings, both good and evil, crowded about Him. For four thousand years Satan had prepared for the imminent encounter in the wilderness. As Jesus prayed for help, the curtain of heaven seemed to part, and a stream of light shone from God's throne to flood with radiance the kneeling form of the Nazarene. Jehovah's majestic voice "resounded through heaven, and echoed through earth like peals of thunder."—Ellen G. White, in *Seventh-day Adventist Bible Commentary*, Vol. 5, p. 1078. It summoned the inhabitants of the universe to mark God's endorsement of the Prince of Paradise by declaring, "This is my beloved Son, in whom I am well pleased." Matthew 3:17.

Immediately from the open heavens "the Spirit of God, like a dove of burnished gold, hovered over the head of Christ."—*Ibid.* Then, "lighting upon him" (verse 16), He found His permanent home in the heart of Christ. The Father and the Spirit, rendezvousing with Christ on planet Earth, joined to sustain the Son of man for His ordeal in the desert.

The divine personages had selected "a bodily shape like a dove" (Luke 3:22), of "purest light" (*The Desire of Ages*, p. 112), to symbolize the Holy Ghost. The dove came upon Jesus as God's assurance of His Sonship and as Heaven's witness before men and angels that the Son of man, the Saviour of the world, had been commissioned for His task.

Undisturbed and at peace, the Dove of God found His permanent home in the Saviour's life. With loving eyes, limpid as a dove's, the Spirit had searched out His Beloved, and nothing would now drive Him from His rest. Vibrant with life, He shared His life. Warm with love, He fluttered down and warmed the Beloved. Shimmering with heaven's beauty, He flew, spreading a beauty not of this world. Messenger of God, He served as Interpreter of the intent of that message.

Glory and acceptance, light and assurance, power and communication, come into our longing souls also on the wings of Heaven's Dove. The heavenly radiance which fell on Christ will fall on every individual who prays for help to resist temptation. God still says of every believer, "This is my beloved child, in whom I am well pleased."—Ellen G. White, in *Seventh-day Adventist Bible Commentary*, Vol. 5, p. 1079.

We should always make Charles Wesley's petition that of our own:

> "Heavenly, all-alluring Dove,
> Shed Thy overshadowing love,
> Love, the sealing grace impart,
> Dwell within our single heart."

God's Ambassador granted Him permanent authorization and assurance, as He abode in the heart of the Son of God. Choosing to veil His glory in the form of a dove of shimmering gold, He suggests the meekness and humility, the gentleness and guilelessness of dim and fragrant glades. Let us ponder some ideas suggested by the bird of divine omen.

The dove is one of the most appealing Scriptural symbols representing the Holy Spirit. When seeking a dwelling, he flies to the darkest foliage of trees or clefts of rocks. From his secluded retreat, his plaintive call is heard, and all the while he remains unseen. Likewise, in the depths of consciousness, God's Spirit converses with man's spirit. Remaining unseen, the "still small voice" calls as "deep calling unto deep."

Solomon considered the dove an emblem of affection. The Beloved, who is Christ the Bridegroom, looks at His spouse, the church, with "the eyes of doves by the rivers of waters, washed with milk, and fitly set." (Song of Solomon 5:12.) Love-light glistens in His eyes as the charms of His dear one ravish Him. Her shining eyes, as the limpid eyes of a dove, look back at her Lover. An unknown Hebrew poet long ago sang of this love, "As the wings of doves over their nestlings, . . . so are the wings of the Spirit over my heart."

The dove is believed to mate for life. He has eyes for none other than his beloved. We, too, should cultivate the "eyes of a dove," for Solomon compares the bride's heart with the immaculate nature of the constant dove. (Song of Solomon 5:2.) The Christian must maintain this relationship to his Lord, who bestows the Spirit to cement this compact. Nothing but infidelity, the final, continued rejection of His affectionate appeals, will drive the Spirit from our hearts and minds.

The dove's plumage shimmers with iridescence as the sun dances on his feathers. The beauty of the Spirit shines in all its splendor as He reflects the wonders of the heavenly world through the bright rays of the Sun of Righteousness. This covering of glory and love He is ready to develop in the surrendered life. We should ever sing:

> "Come, Holy Spirit, Heavenly Dove,
> With all Thy quickening powers;
> Come, shed abroad a Saviour's love,
> And that shall kindle ours."
> —*Isaac Watts.*

Upon the flat roofs of Palestinian homes, the family often stacks broken pieces of earthenware that form small caves in which pigeons roost. Black with soot on the outside they present a dismal picture indeed; yet from their dark recesses flutter the beautiful birds. Soaring into the bright sky they tumble and cavort in ecstasy. The psalmist sang of these, "Though ye have lien among the pots, yet shall ye be as the wings of a dove covered with silver, and her feathers with yellow gold." Psalm 68:13. The broken pottery embedded on the tops of walls collected dirt, but the roosting doves remained undefiled. Their environment mattered not. As they rose into the sunlight, only their loveliness was seen. The Spirit is ready to make His dwelling in any heart that invites His presence, however sinful it may appear. Ever the *Holy* Spirit, He spreads His own holy character to those who behold His beauty and purity.

The dove personifies kindness. Whenever the Spirit takes possession of the garden of the soul, one of the earliest fruits which He causes to flourish is "gentleness." (Galatians 5:22.) Christ compared the modesty of the Christian with the harmlessness of the dove (Matthew 10:16), and David exulted in God, whose gentleness had made him great (Psalm 18:35). The pres-

Dove of Gold—Ambassador of God

ence of the subduing Spirit in the citadel of the human will marks out the path to greatness in the sight of Heaven.

The psalmist longed for the swiftness of the dove so that he, too, might fly safely to his roost and find rest. (Psalm 55:6.) This desire is all the more significant because of the dove's ability to fly great distances, for neither stormy weather nor mountain barriers deter him. The prophet Isaiah underlines this homing instinct. Through pathless skies, unmindful of storm and darkness, the dove unerringly flies back to his window. (Isaiah 60:8.) In like manner nothing prevents the Spirit from reaching a yearning soul who has prepared Him a home.

The dove signifies the Spirit's life-giving power. A bird hovers over his mate to share his life. At creation the Spirit fluttered upon the waters, thus communicating vital power which enabled life to spring up. Jesus observed that "it is the spirit that quickeneth." (John 6:63.) The various life-forces we witness working in nature all stem from the Holy Spirit by whom "they are created." Paul, too, recognized that "the Spirit is life." (Romans 8:10.) Wherever God's Spirit is present, life springs up. The laws of nature are the power lines for the operations of the Spirit, and he who has the Holy Ghost in his heart has the life of God in his soul. Charles Wesley wrote with wonderful insight:

> "Expand Thy wings, celestial Dove,
> Brood o'er our nature's night;
> On our disordered spirits move,
> And let there now be light."

As the Spirit energizes all nature, so all religious life springs from Him. We who would live for Christ must be, as was our Lord Himself, "born . . . of the Spirit." (John 3:3, 5.) The hovering Dove of burnished gold brought Heaven's assurance that the life of God permeated His Son. Today, as in the baptismal scene of long ago, the dovelike Spirit imparts dovelike characteristics to those of whom the Voice says, This is My beloved son or daughter.

The story of the virgin Mary illustrates this truth. In response to her question, "How?" Gabriel answered, "The Holy Ghost shall come upon thee, and [that is to say] the power of the Highest shall overshadow thee: therefore also that holy thing which shall be born of thee shall be called the Son of God." Luke 1:34, 35. The Spirit implants in the heart of the believer the seed of the divine nature, thus giving birth to a new being which has "escaped the corruption that is in the world through lust." (2 Peter 1:4.) Similarly, our souls should cry, How? and then respond as did Mary, "Behold, the bondmaid of [the] Lord; be it to me according to thy word." Luke 1:38, The Interlinear Literal Translation of the Greek New Testament.

After the Flood, Noah sent out a dove to explore the land. At first she found no place to rest because of the troubled waters and so returned to the ark. Sometimes the Dove of God, too, finds no resting-place in the disturbed waters of passion and conflict. The carnage of the field of battle attracts the vulture, yet repels the dove.

But Noah persisted and released the dove a second time. Eventually the questing bird found a sprouting olive tree. Above the waters of judgment she saw this emblem of victory. This she plucked and brought to Noah, the father of righteousness, as a guarantee of the life which lay beyond. The olive leaf spoke of the joy of the abundant new life springing up in a land which God was restoring. Only Heaven's Dove has seen this promise nearing fulfillment, and He alone can reveal its wonders and give the weary the sign of renewal.

On her third voyage the dove located a place of rest upon the earth and built her nest. Today the Spirit can find no abiding place in a heart not stayed upon Christ. But leaving the ark of God's presence, the heavenly Dove will gladly spread encouragement and peace to all who receive Him. Bringing the olive leaf of Heaven's covenant promises, He will remain in hearts prepared to accept Him.

As He opened His ministry with a prayer of commitment on the banks of Jordan, so the Saviour completed His ministry with another prayer of dedication in the shadows of Gethsemane. Then His face, bearing marks of His ordeal, yet reflected calmness and faith, for He had made His final decision to move toward Golgotha. Rousing His disciples, who had been sleeping in the shade of the garden, Jesus walked toward the coming mob, eventually meeting them face to face. His fearful disciples, torn between a desire to help and an urge to flee, left Jesus alone. There He stood unmoved before His angry enemies bent on His arrest.

"Whom seek ye?" He calmly inquired. "Jesus of Nazareth," one excitedly responded. "I am!" the Saviour, who was Jehovah, replied with dignity. "As these words were spoken, the angel who had lately ministered to Jesus moved between Him and the mob. A divine light illuminated the Saviour's face, and *a dovelike form overshadowed Him*. In the presence of this divine glory, the murderous throng could not stand for a moment. . . . The angel withdrew, and the light faded away."—*The Desire of Ages*, p. 694. (Italics supplied.)

After this exhibition of His position and power, Jesus waited calmly. At this juncture the Spirit, who, as a dove, identified the Saviour at His baptism in water in Jordan, returned once more to identify the Messiah at His baptism of blood in Gethsemane. Again the dove of burnished gold rested on the Saviour's head. God's Ambassador, the glorious and gentle bird, brought assurance to His Son, and evidence to man of Jesus' nature. Heaven seemed to be sending the dove with an olive leaf to those who might desire to know that the storms of judgment were actually over. Christ had virtually won the battle. He had already paid the penalty in the promise and purposes of God, and now Heaven assured believing men of peace through the Prince of

Peace. But none in the garden had eyes to see, and so the darkness of eternal night settled on the unholy mob, while the fears of unbelief blinded the disciples.

The explorer Amundsen trekked to the pole long years before adventurers enjoyed the help of the radio. C. G. Brownlee remembers that on one of his trips, he took with him a pet pigeon. After months of silence from the frozen polar regions, Amundsen's wife noticed the bird back on the roof of their home. "He is alive!" she exclaimed in joy. His representative had come.

Once, long ago, Jesus promised, When I go, I will send My Spirit. On the day of Pentecost the Spirit came. The disciples then knew their Lord had reached His destination. They believed that He sat enthroned at the Father's right hand, for had He not sent His Ambassador to tell them so?

Let us cherish Christ's promise, which is extended to us as well, for just as surely as we do, the Spirit will come into our hearts and abide with us forever, unless we decide to drive Him away. Constantly we should pray with the unknown poet:

> "Holy Spirit, I make Thee welcome,
> Come and be my Holy Guest;
> Heavenly Dove, within my bosom
> Make Thy home and find Thy rest."

2.

MANNA--
Fare of God

The Creator provided Adam with inestimable privileges of sonship—all that his eye could see, his heart might desire, and his hand possess—on one condition—obedience. The discipline imposed by "the tree of the knowledge of good and evil" (Genesis 2:16, 17) was designed to develop and display his love and homage to God, and his generosity and self-control to his fellowmen.

On the point of man's diet Satan attacked God's design and devised his test on our first parents. Adam's relationship to the fruit of the tree decided the direction of his own life and started mankind on the road to sin and ruin. By eating the only forbidden food, a trifle compared with the rich bounties God had generously given, our first parents sowed seeds of rebellion in their own hearts and in the hearts of all their posterity.

After the Flood, God enlarged the list of foods man might eat and warned of dangers lurking along the pathway marked by a disregard of His laws. Notwithstanding this, the first sin recorded after the Deluge depicted this very point. Noah partook of intoxicants, invariably forbidden by our unchanging God, and became drunk. The patriarch's sin thus caused an extension of the original curse to his descendants. (Genesis 9:20-27.) At creation and again after the Flood, man expressed his own willfulness by what he chose to eat in flagrant disregard of Jehovah's expressed command.

Today we still display our attitude to God by our choices of what we eat and drink. Have you ever tried to give an unwilling baby his bottle or a little boy spinach? We eat what we want even as infants! The Lord gave man the opportunity to select his food within the limits of divine suggestions. In this simple way he could identify his will with that of his Creator, and this path is still open to us. The Lord imposed basic rules to see "whether . . . [man would] keep his commandments, or no." (Deuteronomy 8:2, 16; compare with Exodus 16:4.) By failing to curb the appetite, man brought damnation upon the whole race.

Soon after leaving Egypt, the Israelites found themselves in the inhospitable wilderness. They did not so choose; their position resulted from their fulfilling the Lord's command. With adequate stocks of food they, at first, felt no need and faced the future with great confidence. But when, after a few weeks, they had used up their resources, God allowed them to come into actual want. Then, and only then, the hand of Jehovah fed them. He purposed that His people should ever ground their trust upon His promises. .

In their desperation Israel doubtingly asked, "Can God furnish a table in the wilderness?" Psalm 78:19. In response, the Lord demonstrated His power and showed them His love. "When all means of sustenance failed, God sent His people manna from heaven; and a sufficient and constant supply was given. This provision was to teach them that while they trusted in God and walked in His ways, He would not forsake them."—*The Desire of Ages*, p. 121. As in the previous typical experiences following Creation and the Deluge, this gift of heavenly food also tested their loyalty to Him.

The provision of manna involved more than the meeting of

mere physical needs. The food provided for Adam and Eve in the Garden of Eden existed before God had created them, and He designed it to strengthen them to fulfill the purpose for their being. The provisions given to take on board the ark had grown in the world that existed before the Flood. These tided them over the first months of need following the desolations of that convulsion. In the wilderness manna came from Paradise, springing from another world. Supplied from heaven by angels, it should surely have adequately met man's needs.

But Jesus observed to the Jews, "Your fathers did eat manna in the wilderness, and are dead." John 6:49. Even "the corn of heaven" did Israel no lasting good. God purposed that they should eat it and gain strength to enter the land of promise. But Israel neither gave thanks to their Provider, nor carried out His will in appreciation for His blessing. So their "carcases fell in the wilderness." (Hebrews 3:17.)

God granted manna as a gift. Man had not plowed or sown to raise it, yet its coming did not license laziness. God required Israel to gather His bounty daily. They might obtain more luxuries from the earth, but the staff of life came from God Himself. Those who refused it perished.

Jesus reminded the Jews that it was not Moses who gave that bread from heaven. "The giver of the manna was standing among them," Ellen White declared most revealingly. "It was Christ Himself who . . . daily fed them with the bread from heaven. *The life-giving Spirit, flowing from the infinite fullness of God, is the true manna.*"—*The Desire of Ages,* p. 386. (Italics supplied.) Manna symbolizes the Holy Spirit, who comes to needy men at the Saviour's behest.

Nehemiah apparently understood this meaning. He called attention to the Spirit's special functions in this triplet of Hebrew poetry: "Thou gavest also thy good *spirit* to instruct them, and withheldest not thy *manna* from their mouth, and gavest them *water* for their thirst." Nehemiah 9:20. If this is Hebrew synonymous parallelism, each of these phrases expands the idea contained in the others. The Spirit's functions are illustrated by manna and water.

Manna always remained mysterious, and its name, "What is it?" (the Hebrew in Exodus 16:15, margin, and R.S.V.) crystallized this idea. None knew whence it came, or whither it went when not used. Moses had spent forty years in the wilderness and probably knew every desert plant. Had manna been the gum or fruit of a shrub, he certainly would not have termed it unknown. But because the people had no idea of its nature, they called it "what's it?" *(man hu')*. Israel daily benefited by eating the manna, but it nonetheless posed mysteries which they could not penetrate. The Christian, too, may enjoy the ministry of the Spirit in his life without understanding much connected with the nature and relationships of the third Person of the Trinity.

Moses reminded the Israelites that God "fed thee with manna . . . that he might make thee know that man doth not live by bread only, but by every word that proceedeth out of the mouth of the Lord doth man live." (Deuteronomy 8:3.) The Holy Spirit today helps spiritual Israel to look beyond the material things to the things of eternity. He inspired the writers of the Bible (2 Peter 1:21), and only as we learn its message can we gain living faith. After man has once feasted on the Scriptures, the Spirit daily helps him meet his problems by bringing the words of life to his remembrance. Israel received this instruction through the manna.

Manna fell with the dew. Each morning it appeared as the hoarfrost, white and shining. (Exodus 16:13, 14.) As regularly as did the sparkling dew, this "manna continued to fall, and they were fed by a divine hand morning and evening."—Ellen G. White, *Testimonies*, Vol. 3, p. 340.

But God's people were required to gather manna promptly, for when the sun rose, it vanished like frost. "Are all the members of your church seeking to gather fresh manna every morning and evening?" the servant of the Lord asks. "Are you seeking divine enlightenment?"—*Ibid.*, Vol. 5, p. 486. Before the heat and burdens of the day, the dew fell gently, silently, bringing the life-forces of nature into action. So God's Spirit stands ready to strengthen the faithful Christian before he takes up each day's tasks. Let us ever pray:

> "Drop Thy still dews of quietness,
> Till all our strivings cease,
> Take from our souls the strain and stress,
> And let our ordered lives confess
> The beauty of Thy peace."
>
> —*John G. Whittier.*

Manna resembled the color of bdellium or, as Moffatt renders the Hebrew, a "pearl." (Numbers 11:7.) Like frost, its purity covered the ugliness of earth with the beauty of snow. The surface of a pearl, like the smear of oil on a puddle, acts like a prism. As the sun falls on the nacre, its light is broken up into a thousand shimmering rays. Jesus is called "the Sun of righteousness." The Holy Ghost now demonstrates to us the radiance of His life in all its loveliness by revealing to every longing heart the beauties of God's true Light. (1 Corinthians 2:10-16.)

Manna marked the Sabbath. For almost forty years, or 2,000 weeks, it fell each day, but on the recurring Sabbaths there was none. Israel's attitude toward the manna demonstrated their willingness or otherwise to obey God's law. On the day before the Sabbath, later called the preparation day, twice as much manna fell as on other days. (Exodus 16:4, 22-30.)

The Lord gave His people this double portion on Friday to tide them over the special needs of the weekend. Each preparation day the message of the manna to Israel was, Get ready for the Sabbath. Do you gather a double portion of His Spirit's power each Friday to help you to "remember the sabbath day to keep it holy" and to worship your Creator?

Some among the Israelites refused to submit to God's plan, and their rebellion soon came to light. Their attitude toward this divinely appointed food revealed their actual relationship to Jehovah. (Verse 27.) As with Adam and Eve, and later with Noah, and now with Israel, subordination of man's appetite to God's will clearly indicated their true condition. By observing the Sabbath carefully, the people of Israel demonstrated that the Word of God ruled their lives. But some ignored both Jehovah's command and promise and went out on the Sabbath to gather manna. Thinking only of temporal food, they demonstrated their disregard of the Lord's express will and their distrust of His power.

Through the manna the Lord worked a threefold miracle each week. A double portion fell on the sixth day, *reminding* them of the fourth commandment. None fell on the Sabbath, *warning* them to do no work on that day, even to provide food. God preserved Friday's portion fresh and enabled it to meet the needs of the Sabbath also, *assuring* them of His faithfulness and keeping power.

Besides all this, manna convicted them of *sin* by pointing to God's command. It underlined righteousness, by insisting on implicit obedience, and by removing all excuse for disobedience. When Jehovah commanded Israel to stone a Sabbathbreaker for his flagrant flaunting of His law, manna pointed to an inevitable judgment. The Spirit now performs this threefold ministry for Christians by convincing us of sin, righteousness, and judgment. (John 16:8-11.)

God granted Israel manna only when they were humble and hungry. (Deuteronomy 8:3.) Given to meet man's need, it taught a vital lesson: only when man cries to God for aid will he receive the heavenly Bread. Christ will not thrust His Spirit on the proud and self-satisfied. Indifference grieves away the Holy Ghost.

Manna lasted only for a day at a time to supply the needs of him who gathered it. The years of Israel's desert wandering typify our earthly pilgrimage. The Promised Land points to Paradise. "For forty years they were daily reminded by this miraculous provision, of God's unfailing care and tender love."—Ellen G. White, *Patriarchs and Prophets*, p. 297. Today the Spirit is our provision. But remember, this abundance, though lasting through all those years, came only in daily portions. God's gifts are always so. "As thy days, so shall thy strength be" (Deuteronomy 33:25), He promises. He has resources to sustain His people as long as they live, yet He gives His Spirit to each of us adequate for our daily needs.

Each individual had to gather his daily manna. He who gathered not went hungry. Paul endorsed the idea that the man who fails to work should starve. (2 Thessalonians 3:10.) The lazy or disobedient among the Israelites tried to obtain a sufficient supply for several days. But the manna not used on the day collected "bred worms, and stank." (Exodus 16:20.) To hoard it was to lose it. Realizing this, we should constantly pray, "Give us day by day [or, for the day, margin] our daily bread." Luke 11:3. It is a fatal blunder to rely on strength gained in experiences with God's Spirit yesterday to help in tomorrow's conflicts. Our experience with His victorious grace today should encourage us to seek for even more tomorrow.

In the days of Moses, each man measured the manna he had gathered, and when he tallied what he had collected, each had precisely an omer. Out of the thousands of Israel every person always had a sufficient quantity at the end of the transaction. (Exodus 16:16-18.)

Christ, the Word Incarnate, provides the Word Inspired. We should "eat" these words, making them part of our lives, by complying with their requirements. Every man in Israel was granted manna "according to his eating." While God provided much more than His people could possibly use, the individual appetite governed the individual amount of blessing each received. As we desire, so shall we receive the Spirit.

The psalmist called manna the "corn of heaven." (Psalm 78:24.) Everyone, in whatever state of need, ate the same manna. God did not adapt it to differing palates. He regarded it as adequate for all. "Sustained by 'the corn of heaven,' they were daily taught that, having God's promise, they were as secure from want as if surrounded by fields of waving grain on the fertile plains of Canaan."—*Patriarchs and Prophets*, p. 297. Grains contain the elements of nutrition, but man must make the staff of life from them. As manna provided Israel with what they needed, so the Holy Ghost gives to the Christian all the vital elements which enable him to live a healthy spiritual life.

Manna was small. Although necessary, one might easily despise it. As we shall see, Inspiration likens the ministry of the Spirit to a "still small voice," a soft evening zephyr, the gentle dew, the small showers on the mown grass, and the gentle dove. The manna of the Spirit is omnipotent to bring within the reach of finite man infinite resources.

Although manna melted in the sun, it was hard enough to grind. (Numbers 11:8.) Durable for its intended use, it disappeared when neglected. The Spirit is mighty enough to bring cosmos out of chaos, and yet the weakest sinner can thwart His working and render impotent the power of heaven by *grieving* Him away. (Ephesians 4:30.)

Manna fell about each tent. God reduced the distance needed to gather it to a minimum. The most feeble needed only to open his tent door to find all he required. So His Spirit is always by us. "The Lord is nigh," the psalmist exulted. (Psalm 34:18; compare with Deuteronomy 4:7.) Through His Representative Christ comes closer to us than breathing and feeling. Stretch out your hand of faith, and receive Him! Fill yourself with His fullness! If any man perishes, he does so within reach of God's abundant Spirit.

It seems incredible, but some loathed the manna! (Numbers

Manna—Fare of God

21:5.) As it cost Israel nothing, some valued it little. What a strange paradox! God's choicest gift we often regard lightly. Mortal man despised the corn of heaven. Today we either take God's good Spirit and love and cherish and obey Him, or we loathe His presence and trample Him under the feet of our neglect or rejection.

But manna did not nauseate the faithful. For almost forty years the true, trusting, grateful people of God rejoiced in His blessings and grew strong by His bounties. Today the ministry of the Spirit completely satisfies the souls and challenges the minds of all who simply and joyfully receive Him as Guide of their lives and Bread of their souls.

Manna was not an afterthought, but existed before Israel needed it. The Holy Spirit is eternal, and His resources completely adequate. Man's emergencies exist only in the limitation of human understanding. God continued sending Israel manna until the wilderness wandering ended. Christ has promised us, "Lo, I am with you alway, even unto the end of the world." Matthew 28:20. His Spirit will continually minister His gifts to the needy church until we all reach perfect unity and fitness for a place in God's kingdom. (Ephesians 4:13.)

Manna ceased only when Israel entered Canaan. (Joshua 5:11, 12.) The Holy Ghost, the great Archetype of the manna, will continue to enable us to live the pilgrim life of faith here on earth until we enter the gates of God's city. Israel's reliance upon supernaturally bestowed manna eventually gave place to confidence in the naturally ripening corn of Canaan. So the Christian will nourish himself in the Spirit until finally led to the fullness of joy face to face with God in the hereafter.

We should pray, "Nourisher of God, ravish our souls with the fare of heaven."

3.

SALT --
Preserving of God

Salt, an essential element for the preservation of life, is popularly used in all lands. In every kitchen and on every table it adds flavor and zest as it mingles with various foods and quietly accomplishes its purpose. Salt inhibits decay. When once blended with the food, it becomes invisible.

It is useless for salt to remain by itself; it must penetrate and pervade what it is to benefit. Carried in solution to every particle, it imbues each fragment with itself. The salt, independent of any value in the things salted, contributes quality and flavor and resistance to decay.

Ellen White long ago observed: "The Spirit . . . is compared to salt, because of its preserving qualities."—*Testimonies*, Vol. 4, p. 319. Let us consider the reasons why Inspiration employs this symbol. Our study will aid our understanding of still another aspect of the Spirit's ministry.

Like salt, the Spirit must permeate and fill the life of the true disciple. (Ellen G. White, *Thoughts From the Mount of Blessing*, p. 36.) Only then will the Christian's influence flavor and preserve his community. This pervasive presence of the Holy Spirit makes the Christian the salt of the earth. For this reason, "unless

SALT—PRESERVING OF GOD 27

the Holy Spirit can use us as agents through whom to communicate to the world the truth as it is in Jesus, we are as salt that has lost its savor and is entirely worthless."—*Ibid.*, p. 37. "The Holy Spirit is to animate and pervade the whole church, purifying and cementing hearts."—*Testimonies*, Vol. 9, p. 20. Before the disciple can fulfill Heaven's plan for his life, the Spirit must influence all his thinking and acting.

In likening His disciples to "the salt of the earth" (Matthew 5:13), Jesus stressed a special ministry of the Holy Spirit. Ellen White observes, "The savor of the salt represents the vital power of the Christian—the love of Jesus in the heart, the righteousness of Christ pervading the life. The love of Christ is diffusive and aggressive. If it is dwelling in us, it will flow out to others. We shall come close to them, till their hearts are warmed by our unselfish interest and love. The sincere believers diffuse vital energy, which is penetrating and imparts new moral power to the souls for whom they labor. It is not the power of the man himself, but the power of the Holy Spirit that does the transforming work."—*Thoughts From the Mount of Blessing*, p. 36. The Christian's influence, like salt, pervades his neighborhood when infused in his heart.

Salt was used in Old Testament times in connection with the birth of a baby. In discussing the origin of Israel, God compared His people with a little girl. He noted that her parents had neglected her. "As for thy nativity," He reminisced, "in the day thou wast born, . . . thou wast not salted at all." Ezekiel 16:4. The antiseptic qualities of a salt scrub evidently formed part of the preparation of a newborn babe to meet the dangers of life on this planet. Similarly the stimulating power of the Spirit vitalizes the new convert for his life as a Christian.

In the story of the bitter stream at Jericho, salt played a major role and represented the Spirit's transforming power. The prophet Elisha charged the elders of that city who had asked him for help to fetch him a new cruse filled with salt. This he cast into the spring of brackish, useless water. After its source had been purged, the entire stream was immediately sweetened. (2 Kings 2:19, 22.)

This experience explains one way in which God renews the unregenerate soul. All his outward circumstances may appear satisfactory, but unless his heart is radically changed, he remains defiled. The Lord longs to make this transformation. When the disciple yields to the Spirit and is born again and starts out in his new life, he is further "seasoned with salt." The Spirit of God is the agent who brings about this metamorphosis. "All who are born of God will become co-workers with Christ. Such are the salt of the earth. 'But if the salt have lost his savor, wherewith shall it be salted?' If the religion we profess fails to renew our hearts and sanctify our lives, how shall it exert a saving power upon unbelievers?"—*Testimonies*, Vol. 5, p. 389.

Ellen White has pointed out that "the savor of the salt is divine grace."—*Ibid.*, Vol. 3, p. 559. Divine grace acts as an antiseptic in the life. It neutralizes what defiles and destroys the satanic forces which would beguile us and debase our characters. This is the work of the Spirit. He fulfills in us Christ's imperative, "Ye must be born again." John 3:7. Working silently from within, the grace of the Spirit transforms and regenerates.

In the Hebrew system of sacrifices salt is associated with blood. As a result of observing this symbol as used by the Jews, many primitive cultures came to regard salt as a type of the life forces. Physicians sometimes inject a saline solution into the veins of certain sick persons. In the cases of the bitter spring made sweet, the salted babe, as well as in the life of the newly converted, the salt of the Spirit infuses the life of God into the polluted stream of human life. The Spirit makes real the promise, "Whosoever is born of God doth not [habitually] commit sin; for his seed remaineth in him; and he cannot [continually] sin, because he is born of God." 1 John 3:9. But the Christian must choose to yield to the heavenly Helper day by day.

"Have salt in yourselves," Christ concluded one of His discourses, "and have peace one with another." Mark 9:50. The salt of the Spirit in our lives will purify, preserve, and perfect our everyday contacts with each other, and its by-product will be in accord with God and man.

Salt cannot remain isolated from the food into which it is put. Likewise "a man is no sooner converted than in his heart is born a desire to make known to others what a precious friend he has found in Jesus; the saving and sanctifying truth cannot be shut up in his heart. The Spirit of Christ illuminating the soul is represented by the light, which dispels all darkness; it is compared to salt, because of its preserving qualities; and to leaven, which secretly exerts its transforming power."—*Ibid.*, Vol. 4, pp. 318, 319. Check your life, and note carefully whether you possess these Spirit-induced characteristics, and then give yourself in service to others.

Perhaps the simplest way to witness for our Saviour is to reveal His love in our conversation. "Let your speech be alway with grace, seasoned with salt, that ye may know how ye ought to answer every man," Paul recommended. (Colossians 4:6.) Speech communicates, and when the Spirit possesses the tongue, and the savor of divine salt seasons the words, the Christian's conversation will effect goodness. It will build up and not tear down. The salt of the Spirit will slay mere idle and railing words. Foolish talking and jesting will give place to sober and edifying ideas. "The savor of the salt is divine grace. All the efforts made to advance the truth are of but little value unless the Spirit of God accompanies them."—*Ibid.*, Vol. 3, p. 559. The salt of the Spirit should ever pervade our speech.

Salt adds flavor to food. Job inquired, "Can that which is unsavoury be eaten without salt? or is there any taste in the white of an egg?" Job 6:6. Even the provender of cattle was sprinkled with salt. (Isaiah 30:24, margin.) The presence of the Spirit in our food, the Scriptures, makes Bible study stimulating and palatable. Passages which appear dry and uninteresting take on entirely different flavors when the Spirit gives us insight. He who inspired the oracles of God stands ready to stimulate the appetite of the hungry soul as well as spread a banquet before him.

The priests added salt to the burnt offerings to make them acceptable on God's altar. (Ezekiel 43:24.) Salt also made incense efficacious. (Exodus 30:35, margin.) As we present our bodies on God's altar of service—that is, devote our lives to Him— and as our prayers rise to His throne as incense, the salt of the Spirit will make them acceptable.

"In the ritual service, salt was added to every sacrifice. This, like the offering of incense, signified that only the righteousness of Christ could make the service acceptable to God. Referring to this practice, Jesus said, 'Every sacrifice shall be salted with salt.' 'Have salt in yourselves, and have peace one with another.' All who would present themselves 'a living sacrifice, holy, acceptable unto God' (Romans 12:1), must receive the saving salt, the righteousness of our Saviour. Then they become 'the salt of the earth,' restraining evil among men, as salt preserves from corruption (Matthew 5:13)."—*The Desire of Ages*, p. 439.

Salt was also employed to ratify covenants. God gave David the kingdom forever by a "covenant of salt." (2 Chronicles 13:5.) In the same way he had given the priesthood to Aaron centuries before, by a "covenant of salt." (Numbers 18:19.) This concept probably grew out of the idea of hospitality. To share one's salt involved opening one's board for fellowship. The Persian words for *traitor (namak haram)* mean "faithless to salt." (The Hebrew word *melach*, salt, suggests antiseptic durability and pure fidelity.) Once having eaten the food provided by a person, or after having offered him food, enmity must no longer exist. The salt of his host had joined him in a bond of fellowship. So the Spirit longs to bind our lives in tender compacts with heaven and with each other.

Salt is one of the most widely used antiseptic agents. When

SALT—PRESERVING OF GOD 31

the newborn and Spirit-filled Christian begins to live in his community, he will impart the flavoring and preserving influence of the Holy Ghost to all those around him. "Do not withdraw yourselves from the world in order to escape persecution. You are to abide among men, that the savor of divine love may be as salt to preserve the world from corruption. Hearts that respond to the influence of the Holy Spirit are the channels through which God's blessing flows. Were those who serve God removed from the earth, and His Spirit withdrawn from among men, this world would be left to desolation and destruction, the fruit of Satan's dominion. Though the wicked know it not, they owe even the blessings of this life to the presence, in the world, of God's people whom they despise and oppress."—*The Desire of Ages,* p. 306.

Our Lord had all this in mind when He termed His followers the "salt of the earth." "If you are salt, saving properties are in you, and the virtue of your character will have a saving influence."—*Testimonies,* Vol. 6, p. 259. The Christian is God's salt box! What a privilege! Every time we sit down to eat, we should momentarily recall these thoughts regarding salt. May the salt of the Spirit flavor and preserve our lives.

4.

SEAL --
Signet of God

Seals date from antiquity. Descending from the mists of Sumerian history through the decline of Roman civilization, they are employed even in our day. In Biblical times, kings, merchants, and wealthy persons used seals. These were made of bone, metal, stone, porcelain, or terra-cotta. A few were even carved in wood or ivory. Impressed on soft material and affixed on the door of a tomb, a chest, or a document, the seal called attention to the authority of its user.

When made in the form of rings, seals might be set with precious or semiprecious stones or precious metals. Some seals were conical or cylindrical; others round and flat. Many Egyptian seals resembled the form of the scarab beetle, thus adding the element of sacredness to the idea of authority.

Highly prized by their owners, seals were often worn on the fingers in the form of ring stones, or drilled and strung on a cord or chain and draped around the neck. (Song of Solomon 8:6, which speaks of a seal upon the heart, that is, hung upon the breast.) Seals were occasionally worn as bracelets.

Sometimes carved simply with the owner's name and station, and at other times engraved with inscriptions and pictures of ani-

Seal—Signet of God

mals, reptiles, birds, trees, flowers, or vines, the design depicted the position and power of the person represented. The owner regarded his seal as one of his most precious possessions and carefully preserved it.

The earliest material used as the medium for sealing was probably clay. This was impressed with the design by squeezing or rolling the seal into it while it was still soft. The clay then hardened in the sun. Wax and lead were also used. When someone desired to shut a door or a chest, he stretched a cord across or around it and affixed a seal at each end. Pilate probably secured Christ's tomb in this way. A document was often bound and sealed in a similar manner. Archaeologists have discovered many seals with the marks of such cords, or the ridges of papyrus from scrolls still visible in them. Certain seals were dipped in ink or pigment, and the design "printed" on the object. One of Ezekiel's visions illustrated this method of sealing. He heard a man with a writer's inkhorn commanded to set a mark on the foreheads of certain men in anticipation of the day of judgment. (Ezekiel 9:3, 4.) This sealing by the Spirit identifies those who are pure and acceptable in God's sight.

The word most frequently used for "seal" or "sealing" in the Old Testament is rendered by our word *signet*. It was evidently a signet ring or some other kind of sealing apparatus. Jezebel used Ahab's seal to authorize the murder of Naboth. (1 Kings 21:8.) Here the same word appears.

The Greek for seal in the New Testament suggests a marriage contract. The bride's ring symbolically seals her to her husband in wedlock. (Moulton and Milligan, *The Vocabulary of the Greek Testament*, p. 618.) But the word has other uses, such as bond or impression. By extension it also indicates baptism. Through this rite the candidate is sealed, or wedded, to God. The presence of the Spirit in our hearts is evidence of our acceptance as Christ's bride and of our fitness for the marriage of the Lamb.

In the story of the returning prodigal, the father presents a ring to his son. (Luke 15:22.) (The Greek word is different, but its meaning is similar to the usual word for seal.) This gift gave evidence of his complete reinstatement in his father's family. Pharaoh's signet ring, centuries before, had empowered Joseph to act with the full authority of the throne of Egypt. (Genesis 41:42.) The sealing of the Spirit declares that we have been elevated to the relationship of dignity and privilege of sons and daughters of God and that He has authorized us to act by authority springing from this position.

In summary, the words for seal in both Testaments signify a ring or some apparatus for sealing, a bond, an impression, a silver seal, even a parcel of ground (which now belongs to its owner), or the bride's marriage band. The authority of the person whom it represented gave the seal its value and effectiveness. From his position as owner or lord stems the idea of possession or power to impose his right. Out of this grew certain basic concepts fundamental to many social, business, and governmental relationships. All these the seal symbolized. Let us now examine some ideas suggested to us by Heaven's sealing of God's children with the Spirit.

Pharaoh sealed Joseph. Jehovah places His seal upon His people. The father sealed the prodigal. In each case the superior seals the lesser. God the Father seals His incarnate Son. He also seals all His sons and daughters. Paul underlines this thought in his Epistle to the Ephesians. After greeting the believers, the apostle naturally moves into a recital of the activities of God on behalf of His people. The Father blesses and chooses them as His own. He adopts them into His family and accepts them completely; He redeems them in their lost state, forgives their sins, and overflows grace into their lives. He then reveals His plan to gather the Jews and the Gentiles into one family and to work out His purposes for them. He shows His desire that His saints should glorify Him through Christ. After all His family have committed themselves to Him in trust and are sealed, He will come again

Seal—Signet of God

and take final charge of them as His possession purchased long before on Calvary. (Ephesians 1:3-14.)

Seals identify. A seal found by Woolley at a royal burial site at Ur of the Chaldees led to a most interesting discovery of the identity of the buried person. The archaeologist picked up a carved stone which had been flung into the grave pit as the soil was being filled in. At the climax of the excavations, the whole funerary plan spread before the searchers. A vast complex of skeletons, men and women and horses, lay all around. Trappings of gold and precious stones were arranged in orderly array. All this might have remained a mystery unsolved. But when the name of Queen Shub-ad was read on the lapis lazuli seal, the wealth and ritual of the last rites, the multitudes of retainers and pet horses slain, all were explained. (Sir Leonard Woolley, *Ur of the Chaldees*, pp. 44-64.) Seals make identification certain.

The Bible foretells that angels will gather the ripened sheaves of earth, God's saints, in the final harvest. Some of these have long lain in the dust. The celestial harvesters look for the seal of God on them. This distinguishes between the good and the bad grain. To the ignorant and uninitiated Shub-ad's seal contained nothing but irregular strokes, but to him who understood its language, it spoke a clear message. "Nevertheless the foundation of God standeth sure, having this seal, The Lord knoweth them that are his." 2 Timothy 2:19. The Spirit's seal will identify God's faithful people.

The seal marks the believer as the object of special providential care and protection. Ellen G. White asks and answers the question: "What is the seal of the living God, which is placed in the foreheads of His people? It is a mark which angels, but not human eyes, can read; for the destroying angel must see this mark of redemption. The intelligent mind has seen the sign of the cross of Calvary in the Lord's adopted sons and daughters. The sin of the transgression of the law of God is taken away. They have on the wedding garment, and are obedient and faithful to all God's commands."—*Seventh-day Adventist Bible Commentary*, Vol. 7, p. 968. Jesus our Example was marked by God's seal. There was never any doubt about His Sonship or His divine nature. In the same manner the Holy Spirit seals the consecrated disciple as God's child.

The seal implies obligation. When a manufacturer places his seal on his product, he gives assurance that he has reached a certain standard of quality. The seal guarantees that he has carried out the conditions. This is the meaning of the covenant which the priests and Levites drew up and sealed at the time of the return from exile. (Nehemiah 9:38.)

Dough was, on occasion, put into pans containing a trademark. The loaf was baked with the seal of its maker pressed into it. This marked its quality. The Mishnah calls the baker a "sealer" for this reason; he left his stamp on his bread so that others would recognize and acknowledge him as its maker. Jesus is the "bread which came down from heaven." The Father impressed His image on His Son and expressed His character through Him. He who recognizes the Son will also recognize the Father. All who will understand can know the Bread of life. The hallmark of divinity rests upon Him. The presence of the Spirit marks every aspect of His life.

A seal proves ownership. In the days of the Apostle Paul, the timber merchants of Ephesus often purchased trees standing in the forest. They went through the woods marking the ones they desired. Later lumberjacks searched the woods, and whenever they saw the sign on a tree corresponding with the seal they carried, they felled it. Dragging it out, they transported the log to its destination. In this case the seal pledged delivery of the object purchased. God daily marks His followers with His seal. Jesus promised that at the final reckoning He would send His angels to gather home His redeemed. The reward for those who have faithfully served Him here will be everlasting life. The seal of the Spirit is God's guarantee that we belong to Him. The

Seal—Signet of God

basis of our confidence is that "the Lord knoweth them that are his." The authorization of Christ by the Father makes Him the Great Harvester. God has commissioned His bonded Servant to gather Heaven's harvest.

As the owner's sign identified the trees in the Ephesian forest, so each child of God is sealed with his Father's name. No longer does the Christian belong to himself or to the world. He is exclusively the Lord's, and the angelic husbandmen will recognize the mark and carefully garner him at the harvest.

A seal indicates attestation. Letters were often signed by seals and documents made valid by them. The seal indicated the authority of the one who drew up the document. The death decree engineered by Haman was endorsed by the Persian king's seal. (Esther 3:12.) A seal legalized Jeremiah's purchase of land. (Jeremiah 32:10, 44.) This seal guaranteed that the price was sufficient and acceptable to the seller. Darius validated his ordinance to execute Daniel in this way. (Daniel 6:17.) Even divine oracles were sealed so that they might remain unaltered until the time of their application. So with Christ's payment for our redemption. By the gift of the Spirit God attests His acceptance of the believer and His approval of his character. The Holy Spirit bears testimony in our hearts that we are indeed the children of God.

The design on the seal is reproduced in the substance in which the impression is made. Not only does Heaven approve the child of God, but he who is born of the Spirit in turn approves the things of Heaven. Thus the presence of God's sealing Spirit in our lives validates us as spiritual epistles "known and read of all men." (2 Corinthians 3:2.) So we become authorized, accredited representatives of Jehovah.

The Scriptures often use the seal as a token of protection or security. Pilate affixed his seal to Joseph's new tomb. It cried, "Keep off!" While the seal remained unbroken, Jesus was considered safe within. Christ the Lover sang that His bride was "a garden inclosed, . . . a spring shut up, a fountain sealed." (Song of Solomon 4:12.) Nothing must violate her purity. By His "scales" leviathan (possibly the crocodile) is "shut up together as with a close seal." (Job 41:15.) Safe within his armor, he scorns his enemies.

Cyril, of Jerusalem (c. 315-386), pleaded with his hearers to take life more seriously. "Remember the Holy Spirit of whom we have spoken," he cried. "He is ready to seal your soul, and He will give you a seal which devils fear, a seal heavenly and divine. . . . Yet He tries the soul that He seals; He does not cast His pearls before swine. If you play the hypocrite, you may be baptized by men, but you will not be baptized by the Spirit. But if you come in faith, while men will administer the visible rite, the Holy Spirit will give you that which is invisible. You are on the eve of a great crisis in life."—*Catacheses*, XVII, 35.

Legions of angels stand ready to aid the beleaguered soul who bears the protective seal of the Spirit. So long as the relationship suggested by this seal remains intact, the power of Omnipotence makes the soul invincible.

A seal permanently settled a deed of sale while any unsealed transaction was liable to change. We have been bought with a price through the blood of Jesus Christ. When God places the seal of His Spirit upon us, He desires to consummate His plan for our lives. Once He seals the bargain, the merchandise cannot be altered. The characters of those whom He seals remain unchangeable.

Certain conditions are necessary before the material can receive the impress of a seal perfectly. It must be soft and completely yielding. If it resists, like rubber, or contains hard aggregate, like concrete, the impress will be imperfect. The medium must be smooth and consistent within itself, like wax or clay, or even lead. Then it can receive the likeness exactly. "As wax takes the impression of the seal, so the soul is to take the impres-

Seal—Signet of God

sion of the Spirit of God and retain the image of Christ."—Ellen G. White, in *Seventh-day Adventist Bible Commentary*, Vol. 7, p. 970.

There is, of course, a great difference between wax and the soul. The soul can choose either to yield or to resist. Men can reject the pleadings of the Spirit. God may purpose to establish us forever, but we may interpose a perverse will. "The Spirit conforms the renewed soul to the model, Jesus Christ."—Ellen G. White, in *Review and Herald*, August 25, 1896. "If men are willing to be moulded, there will be brought about a sanctification of the whole being. The Spirit will take the things of God and stamp them on the soul."—Ellen G. White, *The Acts of the Apostles*, p. 53. But never forget, the constant choice remains with us!

Another requirement for receiving the seal of God is faith. The Father promised the disciples the Spirit, and Jesus ratified this promise. But the Spirit, sent by the Son from the Father, Paul emphasized, enters the soul only through the exercise of hope, faith, and acceptance on our part. (Ephesians 1:12, 13.)

When the Spirit seals believers, it is with the goal of the day of final reward in mind. The apostle calls this the day of redemption. (Ephesians 1:14; 4:30.) Enoch received the impress of the divine character to keep him safe and was ready for God to take him. Having been sealed, the life of the Christian reflects, albeit dimly, what he will ultimately be. Then the Spirit's continued presence restores the image of God fully in the soul. It helps the Christian to conform daily to the likeness of Christ's character. When this likeness can be discerned, "the Spirit itself beareth witness with our spirit, that we are the children of God."

This reception of a perfect likeness from a seal does not happen in a moment. It is the result of a process. The sealer, for his part, must make his impression, while the wax must remain soft and cooperative. Finally, the wax must set. "Would you impress the seal to obtain a clear impression upon the wax, you do not dash it on by a violent action, but you place the seal carefully and firmly and press it down until the wax receives the mold. Just so the Lord is dealing with our souls. . . . Not now and then, but constantly the new life is implanted by the Holy Spirit after Christ's likeness."—Ellen G. White, *In Heavenly Places*, p. 66.

In the Christian's life, God's Word nourishes all growth. Man responds to its appeals by progressively departing from evil, and God places His seal of ownership on His child. As man continues to yield to the power of divine grace, he obtains that holiness which makes him perfectly acceptable to God, and he ultimately grows like his Father in heaven. Then he reflects the image of Jesus fully, and God will fix his character.

"We may talk of the blessings of the Holy Spirit, but unless we prepare ourselves for its reception, of what avail are our works? . . . Are we seeking for His fullness, . . . the perfection of His character? When the Lord's people reach this mark, they will be sealed in their foreheads. Filled with the Spirit, they will be complete in Christ, and the recording angel will declare, 'It is finished.' "—Ellen G. White, in *Review and Herald*, June 10, 1902. "The seal of the living God will be placed upon those only who bear a likeness to Christ in character."—*Ibid.*, May 21, 1895.

The Holy Spirit wishes to make an exact replica of Christ in the heart. By His transforming grace the disciple will become like Jesus in words and works. The Spirit in the soul produces a daily walk with God. The Holy Spirit seeks to reproduce His own holy character in the heart, warmed and softened by the love of God and joyously surrendered to His influence. Dydimus, an ancient Christian, remarked that "the Spirit is the seal which stamps the divine image on the human soul."—*De Spiritu Sancto*, pp. 34-37.

A comparison of the sealed company of 144,000 with the same group on Mount Zion shows that this symbolic sealing is tantamount to the impressing of the Father's name on their fore-

Seal—Signet of God 41

heads. (Revelation 7:3; 14:1.) When Moses wished to see God's glory, the Lord promised to make all His goodness pass before him. As Moses looked and listened, he received a revelation of the divine name and discovered that it stood for the matchless character of God. (Exodus 33:18; 34:5-7.) When the 144,000 finally have the Father's name imprinted on their minds, they will have been brought into perfect conformity with His character. This the sealing of the Spirit effects by reproducing in the yielded soul a perfect facsimile of the disposition of Christ. "We are to be distinguished from the world because God has placed His seal upon us, because He manifests in us His own character of love."—Ellen G. White, *The Ministry of Healing*, p. 37.

The invisible mark which angels discern sets God's true people apart from the rest of mankind. They have characters indicating their likeness to God's ideal. Paul notes that they "depart from iniquity." (2 Timothy 2:19.) In the prophetic vision they sigh and "cry for all the abominations" done in the land. (Ezekiel 9:4.) When the work of preparation is completed, "all their sins will then be blotted out, and they will be sealed with the seal of the living God."—Ellen G. White, *Early Writings*, p. 48.

Authority, ownership, protection, value, and likeness to God will come with the imposition of the seal of the Spirit in the yielded and softened hearts of Christ's true disciples.

"Even after the saints are sealed with the seal of the living God, His elect will have trials individually. Personal afflictions will come; but the furnace is closely watched by an eye that will not suffer the gold to be consumed. The indelible mark of God is upon them. God can plead that His own name is written there. The Lord has shut them in. Their destination is inscribed—'GOD, NEW JERUSALEM.' They are God's property, His possession."—Ellen G. White, *Testimonies to Ministers*, p. 446.

One day, soon, the cry will resound through the earth: "Behold, the bridegroom cometh." Only those with His seal will be ready to meet Him. Now is the sealing time, the yielding time.

5.

EARNEST --
Dowry of God

Horror filled the hearts of Jacob's sons as they listened to the governor's ultimatum. He would hold Benjamin hostage in Egypt! The prospect of having to tell their aged father that they had left his youngest boy behind in an African prison made even the most callous of them shudder. In a gallant plea to the Egyptian prime minister, Judah declared, "Thy servant became surety for the lad unto my father, saying, If I bring him not unto thee, even I shall bear the blame to my father for ever." Genesis 44:32. Judah had pledged his life in exchange for the life of Benjamin, and we should never overlook this idea in our study of the idea of "surety." The Greek cognate is a transliteration of the Hebrew term and is used three times by the Apostle Paul as an emblem of the Holy Spirit. (2 Corinthians 1:22; 5:5; Ephesians 1:14.) It occurs only here in the New Testament.

The Hebrew verb translated "surety" means to mix or to intertwine, and hence to traffic or to barter. It implied that the purposes of the contracting parties had interlocked. It indicated the taking of a pledge or the becoming of a surety. It also may be rendered "mortgaged." (See Genesis 38:17, 18, 20; Nehemiah 5:3.)

The history of Solomon illustrates this concept and its results. His policy called for treaties of friendship and trade with many neighboring countries. From each of these he accepted a princess. These women came to him as pledges of good faith, and in marrying them, Solomon intertwined his destiny with theirs, as well as the destiny of Israel and the people the women represented. Compacts were thus established.

We find further instance of this custom in the story of the return of the postexilic Jews. The historian deplored the intermarriage of the Lord's people with the inhabitants of Palestine. He recorded that the Hebrews took the daughters of the heathen "for themselves, and for their sons: so that the holy seed have mingled themselves with the people of those lands." (Ezra 9:2.) Here "mingled themselves" suggests a willing entry into mutually pledged relationships with unbelievers. This idea of interlacing interest lies at the root of the Hebrew term.

The gift of the Holy Spirit, as surety, assures us that Heaven is deeply involved in the events of earth. The policies of God should penetrate and intertwine the affairs of men. The Lord stands ready to enter into a covenant relationship with His people and to guarantee it with the gift of His Spirit.

A consideration of the occurrences of this word in the Scriptures provides further shades of meaning. The psalmist, for instance, longed for God to stand surety for him in times of trouble. (Psalm 119:122.) This prayer also constitutes the desire of the faithful in every age. In response to the sinner's need Jesus became the surety of a better covenant for all who would accept Him. (Hebrews 7:22.) He laid down His life for our lives and pledged Himself for our redemption. His Spirit in our hearts guarantees that our Saviour has done just this for each of us.

Hezekiah petitioned the Lord, "Undertake for me." The expression may also be rendered "be thou my surety." (Isaiah 38:14.) The king, desperate because of his sickness, longed for God to take his part and guarantee his life. Job, in his loneliness, appealed to his friend Eliphaz to associate himself with him and cried in anguish, "Who is he that will strike hands with me?" (Job 17:3; "strike hands" is a translation of the Hebrew word elsewhere rendered "surety.") Thus, the Hebrew word generally refers to a pledge and conveys the idea of taking a pledge or going surety for debts, of entering into a pact, or of making an exchange. Other usages indicate the giving of a down payment, the establishing of a mortgage, the accepting of a hostage.

The New Testament word for "pledge," as we have noticed, is a transliteration of the Hebrew term and means "an earnest," a mercantile expression probably adopted by the Greeks and Romans from the Phoenicians, who founded ancient commerce. An earnest was a deposit paid by the purchaser when both he and the seller agreed on the conditions of sale. It bound both parties to carry out their contract. Arabs still use "arraboon" in their business deals; it means down payment. The modern Greek in Cyprus uses this word of an engagement ring, a token that both parties will one day consummate their marriage.

We should carefully note the contrasts between the ideas lying at the heart of the words *pledge* and *earnest*. An earnest is a down payment, or partial payment, *in kind,* and forms an actual part of the obligation itself. It implies that the rest of the payment will be made of the same stuff as the deposit. An earnest never returns to the depositor. A pledge, on the other hand, is something given as a guarantee of good faith to ensure the completion of the agreement. It might be any article of value, and the price, when the article is finally redeemed, may be of a totally different nature. The depositor generally takes back the pledge when he completes the transaction. For instance, Judah temporarily left his signet, bracelets, and staff with Tamar to assure her of his intention to fulfill his promise. He expected these back eventually. (Genesis 38:18, 20, 25.)

When a servant received an earnest, or advance, on his wages, it proved that he had been firmly hired. He would collect the rest of his pay when he completed the task, or when the time for the next installment arrived. To those who are faithful in this present life, the earnest of God's Spirit warrants the fullness of ultimate blessings in the life to come. An earnest thus ratifies a bargain or contract.

To sum up: The Hebrew and Greek for earnest or surety both mean something going before, or given in advance, as an assurance of more to come. The time element is never absent in the concept of these words. The final payment must eventually be made. Earnest constitutes the first installment. While, in this sense, it may be regarded as a pledge, it also forms part of the possession or benefit with which the parties forming a compact are dealing. We must keep in mind these ideas of identity and continuity when we consider earnest as a symbol of the Holy Spirit.

When the Lord promises us the "earnest of the Spirit," He means that He will give us much more of the same Spirit. The Holy Spirit as an earnest differs only in degree from the fullness of the gifts which He guarantees. In a sense analagous to this Paul calls the Holy Spirit "first fruits," the gift of the divine Husbandman. (Romans 8:23.)

It is possible that the Greek term "arrabon" has come, through the Latin "arrha" or "arrhabo," via the Middle French "arrhes" into the provincial English "earls" or "arles-penny," and thence "earnest-penny." "Arles," "arnes," and "ernes" are interchangeable. In Anglo-Saxon, "erno" means to give a pledge. "Ern" or "earnest" is the pledge itself. Wycliffe rendered Paul's Greek word by "ernes" and "eernes." These Middle English words have taken on the terminal "t" and developed into our word *earnest*. (See the article on "earnest" in Skeat, *Etymological Dictionary of the English Language*.)

Ancient notices in the Greek papyri use this technical word in interesting contexts. We read: "Regarding Lampon the mouse-catcher, I paid him for you earnest money [arabona] 8 drachmae in order that he may catch the mice while they are with young." Another entry in an ancient record noted that "earnest money, to be reckoned in the price," had been advanced to dancers for a festival. (Moulton and Milligan, *The Vocabulary of the Greek Testament*, p. 79). These vernacular uses shed light on the New Testament significance of this word.

In ancient British law the conveyance of land or houses required the deposit of an earnest. The seller gave the buyer a clod of earth to demonstrate that he was in earnest. This assured the purchaser that he would receive the rest of the property at the agreed time and for the stipulated price. Sometimes the vendor even presented to the purchaser a bunch of thatch from the roof of his house as an earnest, or "arles."

When a suitor had completed his arrangement for a bride, he gave her parents an earnest of support called a dowry. After the wedding the new wife received this marriage portion from her parents to help in the establishment of the home. Ellen White adds this further statement regarding our heavenly Father's gift to His bride, the church: "The rich dowry of the Holy Spirit will be given, and through its constant supply to the people of God they will become witnesses in the world of the power of God unto salvation."—*Testimonies to Ministers*, p. 50. Christ longs for the time when He and His bride will unite in the marriage of the Lamb, and He has given the dowry of His Spirit as the encouraging pledge that He will fulfill His contract of the everlasting covenant.

The servant of Abraham, Eliezer of Damascus, gave Rebekah tokens, or earnest, from the wealth of his master's heir, Isaac. The grapes, pomegranates, and figs which the spies brought back from Canaan were a foretaste, guarantee, earnest, or assurance of the rich bounties of the Promised Land. These instances add luster to the meaning of the term.

In the three contexts in which *earnest* appears in the New Testament, the Apostle Paul calls attention to three fundamental truths. First, the Holy Spirit is the earnest of the fulfillment of all the promises of God through Christ. (2 Corinthians 1:20-22.) He is our assurance of acceptance by the Lord. He catalyzes our *justification*. Second, the Spirit makes possible the Christian's attainment of God's ideal. This state Paul compares to a spiritual "body," or life everlasting. The Holy Spirit is the Agent who aids in our *sanctification*. (2 Corinthians 5:4, 5.) Third, the Spirit guarantees this exalted inheritance, including the believer's restoration to all the blessings which God has in store for him in the earth made new. He provides the means for our *glorification*. (Ephesians 1:13, 14.) Let us consider in detail the circumstances in each passage which display the shades of meaning of the word as Paul employs it.

The apostle's first use of the word *earnest* deals with justification. His emphasis grows out of his relationship with the believers in Corinth. Paul had promised to visit them as soon as he was able, but circumstances beyond his control had prevented him from carrying out his plan for some long time. His opponents accused him of vacillation, or even prevarication. Paul denied these charges, and in his second Epistle to Corinth he set out the reasons why the delays had been necessary. Paul first demonstrated, in the largest context, that the lives of all Christians rest in God's hands. As the believer submits his will to the Lord, he may sometimes have to alter his own plans, yet the Most High is ever faithful and will ultimately vindicate those who have submitted to His guidance. (1 Corinthians 16:5-7; 2 Corinthians 1:15-20.)

God had, of course, authorized the initial preaching of the gospel in Corinth, and His chosen instruments, Paul, Silvanus (or Silas), and Timothy had carried out the divine plan. They had proclaimed the truth regarding the Messiah, and people had listened and believed. The converts had learned that Christ is never fickle, for in Him God's every promise is a Yea. He stands ready to establish every declaration from the throne of Omnipotence. He makes every divine promise a judicial affirmation and validates it by the final Amen. Sometimes, because of man's obstinacy, God's plans might appear delayed, but, Paul reasoned, He would eventually carry out all His great purposes. Paul and his helpers were part of this overruling scheme, for Heaven had confirmed their actions. So Paul could declare that all the promises of God in Christ were "yea, and in him Amen." The Christian must ever submit his will to the Lord. This, as Paul pointed out, might well mean the waiving of the believer's own plans. Because of all this the apostle's visit had been delayed.

At this stage in his argument Paul drove home his main point by carefully drawing the Corinthian Christians within this large circle. They, with us, with the Father and the Son, were all part of God's developing purpose. The reason for Paul's inability to carry out his design of revisiting the Corinthians was that the Father, Son, and Spirit had willed otherwise. Could he, a mere man, do anything in these circumstances but comply? Christians were separate threads in the tapestry being woven in the loom of Heaven. They must solve their local disappointments by viewing the finished design, for by the bestowal of His Spirit, God was assuring them that everything would ultimately work out for the best. Thus, the earnest of the Spirit was Heaven's down payment, guaranteeing the final carrying out of God's ideal in each life. The Spirit is Heaven's dowry. God will fulfill all His promises to unite His bride with Himself through justification. The Spirit makes the new birth a reality. He said, "Amen!" and sealed the everlasting compact. The gift of the Comforter was God's down payment, pledging that He would also carry out the rest of the contract and bring the faithful to glory.

An earnest was often deposited when uncertainty marked the time for the completion of the transaction. God has promised that one day Christ will return to bestow immortality upon His sons and daughters. We do not know when He will fulfill the promise. The apparent delay in its realization, however, should not discourage the man of faith, even though ignorance of the "times and seasons" may sometimes be frustrating. The earnest of the Spirit's presence should ever assure the trusting heart, for in the end Christ will make all God's promises "yea."

Paul's second illustration deals with sanctification. He observes that the Holy Spirit is the earnest of the Christian's spiritual, or celestial, body, that is, his habitation "eternal in the heavens." He notes that God had created man to attain this high sphere of victorious existence. (2 Corinthians 5:1, 5.) Then Paul underlined another truth. While the believer lives day by day in his fleshy body, he must not allow its upsurging passions and desires to control him. He must resolve to be absent from the downward pull of his base nature and seek to be at home with the Lord, who is ready to live in his heart. J. B. Phillips presents the apostle's case thus: "Now the power that has planned this experience for us is God, and he has given us his Spirit as a guarantee of its truth. This makes us confident, whatever happens. We realize that being 'at home' in the body means that to some extent we are 'away' from the Lord, for we have to live by trusting him without seeing him. We are so sure of this that we would really rather be 'away' from the body and be 'at home' with the Lord. It is our aim, therefore, to please him, whether we are 'at home' or 'away.'" 2 Corinthians 5:5-9. One way of life is on an earthly level. It is tied to the pursuits and passions of the present. God's grace has fashioned the other. In this life, with its problems and temptations, we groan and long for the better things of the next. True Christians desire above all else the appearing of the Lord Jesus Christ, who shall change our existence from glory into glory. (2 Corinthians 5:1-5; compare 1 Thessalonians 4:16-18; 1 Corinthians 15:50-57.)

Many times we tire of our earthly life with its burdens and vexations, Paul suggests, but we should conquer this mental condition, for it actually shows a mistrust of God. Some of us may even tremble at the prospect of death, but this fear is needless, for Christ will fulfill our grandest desires and swallow up death in victory. God created us to attain this very end. He guarantees our triumph by granting us the earnest of His Spirit. When the great controversy ends, an eternal mansion awaits each victor. Although the awesome tribunal of Christ might still intervene, the trusting soul has nothing to fear.

In 2 Corinthians 5:10, 11 Paul stresses the goal of sanctification. The Spirit is God's pledge of this. The presence of the earnest now assures of our being at home with our Saviour in fellowship—a foretaste of that oneness with Him which we shall enjoy for all the ages.

Paul's third use of this word points to glorification. God gives the Holy Spirit as the earnest of our inheritance, for Jesus, the Kinsman-Redeemer, will eventually restore our lost heritage. The Comforter enters our hearts to encourage and sustain us "until the redemption of the purchased possession, unto the praise of his glory." (Ephesians 1:14.) We should view the picture the apostle here paints from two angles, God's and ours. First, the church is God's heritage. He is our owner, for we have been taken as an inheritance. Second, the consummation of the Lord's plan for His people is an eternity of bliss. This constitutes the heritage of the church. The apostle calls this future state "the riches of the glory of his inheritance in the saints." (Ephesians 1:18.) Paul records his conviction that God has destined us, the ransomed saints who have heard and believed the word of truth, to become the cause of "the praise of his glory." (Ephesians 1:12.) One day our Saviour will return for His people, whom He has purchased with His own precious blood, and take them to Himself. The Holy Spirit, the earnest God has left with us, guarantees our ultimate glorification.

It is interesting to observe why the saints' reward is called an inheritance. To have an inheritance one must be an heir, and to be an heir presupposes a relationship. In Christ we are sons and daughters of God, for our Lord has "begotten us again into a lively hope by the resurrection." (1 Peter 1:3.) So Paul sums up: "The Spirit itself beareth witness with our spirit, that we are the children of God: and if children, then heirs; heirs of God, and joint-heirs with Christ." Romans 8:16, 17. This precious promise should buoy us up. For it is equally true of all believers that "if ye be Christ's, then are ye Abraham's seed, and heirs according to the promise." (Galatians 3:29.)

To the child of God "all things are possible." As a brother or sister of Christ we are joint-heirs of all things possessed by our Father. Every advantage the Redeemer obtains, His brethren may also attain. Even in this life we can be "heirs" of "the righteousness which is by faith," which comes to us as a gift from our Lord. (Romans 5:17.) He imputes His righteousness to us day by day as we "grow up into him in all things." To enable us to do this, His Spirit remains with us "till we all come in the unity of the faith, and of the knowledge of the Son of God, unto a perfect man, unto the measure of the stature of the fulness of Christ." (Ephesians 4:13.)

This celestial heritage extends far beyond time for, as Christians, Christ makes us "heirs according to the hope of eternal life." Day by day the Holy Spirit directs angelic ministrants to the aid of all "who shall be heirs of salvation." (Titus 3:7; Hebrews 1:14.)

This vitalizing power, by which alone the Christian maintains his victorious life, comes to him because he is an heir "of the grace of life." Each moment he remains under the guidance of an omnipotent Sovereign. He is an heir of the kingdom established by Christ. Because of this the faithful soul eventually inherits all things, for he is heir of the world to come. As sons and daughters of our heavenly Father, we have access to all the joys and privileges of His home. Our homes on earth and our daily lives should constitute little bits of heaven on earth while we prepare to go to God's eternal heaven. This glorious heritage is not ephemeral, but everlasting, and those of us who respond to God's call "receive the promise of eternal inheritance" and "eternal life." (Hebrews 9:15; John 3:15.)

The Holy Spirit, God's down payment, brings us courage day by day, guaranteeing that the Christian will inherit all things. As we are conscious that Christ, by His Spirit, dwells in our hearts and influences our lives, our eyes should constantly peer beyond the things of time to the things of eternity. All these glorious aspirations are packed into the word *heaven,* for in that better land all that hurts and mars will be forever forgotten. Incorruption will displace the corruption resulting from satanic forces, which destroy body and soul. What is sown in dishonor will rise in honor. The persecuted and downtrodden, the martyred and ignored, will then partake of glory, honor, and immortality. "Sown in weakness; it is raised in power." The crippled and deformed, the war shocked and blasted, will one day arise with "a spiritual body." The earthborn and earthbound will one day wing their way to realms of light and will join with other spirit beings in work and worship. Because "God hath revealed them unto us by his Spirit" (1 Corinthians 2:10), we can see the joys possible to the glorified. The earnest of the Spirit places all these eternal realities within our limited comprehension and empowers us to live, "as seeing him who is invisible." (Hebrews 11:27.)

And so the divine Father has granted us the dowry of the marriage He plans for His Son; He has provided the earnest, guaranteeing His threefold promise. The Spirit is Heaven's deposit assuring the fulfillment of all God's pledges of an eternal heritage. He gives us confidence that Christ will come soon to gather to Himself His treasured bride—His church, you and me—and take us to His celestial home to live with Him forever. The Holy Ghost is God's pledge that our earthly bodies may become holy temples of our living Lord. May we cherish the gift and prepare for the hereafter with the Giver.

6.

OIL --
Luminance of God

In Bible times olive oil provided the main fuel for illumination. The harvesters shook the trees to shed their fruit and then gathered and washed the ripe olives. They placed these in presses to squeeze out the oil, which ran out of the press and was collected in stone or earthenware jars for later use. Sometimes the harvesters trod upon the olives to extract the oil, or on occasion beat it out with rods. This latter method produced the purest, most transparent oil. When they resorted to treading, pulp sometimes rendered the oil opaque. This method, while producing a larger quantity, did not provide for quality. "Pure" olive oil described that which exuded from the ripe berries at the lightest touch. Olive oil symbolizes the Holy Ghost.

The structure of lamps depends on the fuel employed. The seven-branched candelabrum of the sanctuary burned olive oil. For each light there must be a receptacle for the oil. This contained the wick coiled into a narrow space with one end protruding. Capillary attraction constantly drew the oil up to its end. When lighted, the wick provided the vehicle for the oil to burn continuously.

Scripture employs oil as an emblem of a vital aspect of the

working of the Holy Spirit. It suggests the fuel necessary to keep the lamps of Christian witness burning. In Christ's parable, "the wise took oil in their vessels." This was "the grace of God, the regenerating, enlightening power of the Holy Spirit, which renders His word a lamp to the feet and a light to the path."—Ellen G. White, *The Great Controversy*, p. 394.

In the ritual of the Tabernacle, oil played a major role. In Zechariah's vision (Zechariah 4:2-14), the oil for the lamps was stored in a special bowl or vessel. From it the oil flowed to the ends of the seven branches of the lampstand in the holy place. As Zechariah contemplated this beautiful symbol, he could not contain his curiosity. "What be these two olive branches which through the golden pipes empty the golden oil out of themselves?" he asked. We should meditate on the angel's answer to this question. The key is found in verse 6: "Not by might, nor by power, but by my spirit." This vision pictorially represents the extent of the working of the Holy Ghost.

The golden pipes are vehicles through which the oil flows from the bowl to the lamps. "God's people are to be channels for the outworking of the highest influence in the universe. In Zechariah's vision the two olive trees which stand before God are represented as emptying the golden oil out of themselves through golden tubes into the bowl of the sanctuary. From this the lamps of the sanctuary are fed, that they may give a continuous bright and shining light. So from the anointed ones that stand in God's presence the fullness of divine light and love and power is imparted to His people, that they may impart to others light and joy and refreshing. They are to become channels through which divine instrumentalities communicate to the world the tide of God's love."—*Testimonies*, Vol. 6, pp. 11, 12.

Ellen White thus identifies God's people with the golden pipes; they form the channels through whom the golden oil flows to enlighten mankind. She terms this illumination "the highest influence in the universe." Spreading the light is the most im-

Oil—Luminance of God 55

portant function possible for any created being. In the symbolic parts of the Bible, gold typifies faith that works by love. The golden tubes, therefore, picture the human channels in whose lives faith works through the motive of love to spread blessing.

Channels must be clean, or they will defile what passes through them. The Christian's heart must be pure, so as not to mar the influence of Heaven. A golden pipe leads to a lamp; hence each lamp connects with the bowl by its individual line of supply. God purposes that His people shall have a personal connection with the heavenly Source from whom the Holy Spirit flows into life's experience. The Spirit gives His gifts and power "to every man severally as he will." (1 Corinthians 12:11.) This ministry is unique for each individual. God regards each soul with equity, adapting His grace to the personal needs of each.

The golden oil for the lamps has as its immediate source the "bowl of the sanctuary." Thus, in turn, "the two olive trees" constantly replenish this. The two olive trees represent the Scriptures of the Old and New Testaments. (*The Great Controversy*, p. 267.) The Christian gains his knowledge regarding the Spirit and His work through the study of the Bible. Apart from these inspired revelations, the disciple's understanding of the role of the Spirit in his life grows distorted. It is, therefore, vital that the bowl always connect with the two olive trees so that the oil of the Spirit may continue to flow. "Our only safety will be found in constantly seeking wisdom from God, in carefully weighing every matter with much fear and trembling, lest there should be brought into the work not the light of heaven, but the weakness of man."—*Testimonies to Ministers*, p. 211.

The source of supply of the Spirit is limitless. Our Saviour testified, "God giveth not the Spirit by measure." John 3:34. (Weymouth suggests, "in sparing measure.") This may be true for every son and daughter of God.

Notice this most illuminating commentary on Zechariah's vision:

"From the two olive trees, the golden oil was emptied through golden pipes into the bowl of the candlestick and thence into the golden lamps that gave light to the sanctuary. So from the holy ones that stand in God's presence, His Spirit is imparted to human instrumentalities that are consecrated to His service. The mission of the two anointed ones is to communicate light and power to God's people. It is to receive blessing for us that they stand in God's presence. As the olive trees empty themselves into the golden pipes, so the heavenly messengers seek to communicate all that they receive from God. The whole heavenly treasure awaits our demand and reception; and as we receive the blessing, we in our turn are to impart it. Thus it is that the holy lamps are fed, and the church becomes a light bearer in the world."—*Ibid.*, p. 510.

The golden oil, representing the Holy Spirit, constantly supplies God's ministers that they in turn may impart light to the church and the community. Note carefully the stages in this process. God first sends His Spirit into the inspired Scriptures of the Old and New Testaments—the two olive trees, or the two witnesses, or the two anointed ones. From a thorough study of the Scriptures, the dedicated ministry becomes filled with the Spirit. These men are represented by the golden bowl. God designs that the oil shall flow through gold pipes, His delegated and Spirit-filled servants, to the seven lamps or the church in every age and in every place. In this way He empowers His people to shine.

"By the lamps is represented the Word of God."—Ellen G. White, *Christ's Object Lessons*, p. 406. As the individual life of the disciple identifies with the sentiments of Scripture, the Word of God becomes the dynamic of his life. In his body he lives out these heavenly principles day by day. So the lamps may also represent the individual lives of God's people. Solomon observed, "The spirit of man is the candle of the Lord." Proverbs 20:27.

OIL—LUMINANCE OF GOD

The priests tended the lamps each morning and evening. Ellen White has explained this picture. "The lamps of the soul must be trimmed. They must be supplied with the oil of grace. . . . We should daily obtain a deep and living experience in the work of perfecting Christian character. We should daily receive the holy oil, that we may impart to others. . . . From the two olive trees the golden oil flowing through the golden pipes has been communicated to us. But those who do not cultivate the spirit and habit of prayer cannot expect to receive the golden oil of goodness, patience, long-suffering, gentleness, love."—*Testimonies to Ministers*, pp. 510, 511.

Ellen White underscores the need of incorporating the teachings of the Word into the Christian's experience in these words: "By implanting in their hearts the principles of His Word, the Holy Spirit develops in men the attributes of God. The light of His glory—His character—is to shine forth in His followers. Thus they are to glorify God, to lighten the path to the Bridegroom's home, to the city of God, to the marriage supper of the Lamb."—*Christ's Object Lessons*, p. 414.

The Christian must daily make himself empty so that he can be filled with the oil of the Holy Spirit, and so keep burning. The Spirit is ready to maintain, constant and serene, the eternal flame of divine illumination in each Christian's daily experience. . .

The widowed mother, whose sons were to be sold as slaves in order to pay her husband's debts, approached Elisha in her anguish. "What hast thou in the house?" the prophet asked kindly. The memory of her shattered home, through which her creditors had passed seizing everything of value, flashed before her mind. "Not any thing . . . save a pot of oil," she replied bitterly. The prophet could detect a blessing where she could discern only ruin, so he bade her fill her empty house with empty pots! This she did. "Pour out the pot of oil," he directed. And this little remnant of oil filled every vessel she had collected. Only when she had nowhere else to put it, did the oil stop flowing. (2 Kings

4:1-6.) This story underlines the vital truth that the Holy Spirit will cease to flow into our lives only when our capacity to receive Him ends. We limit His power by our desire and ability to be used by Him.

God personally supplies each human lamp with oil. Each has his unique place in space to illuminate, his own function to fulfill. God gives the spiritual oil to each of us to aid in doing our own tasks in life. The Lord called Bezaleel to construct the Tabernacle and "filled him with the spirit of God." (Exodus 35: 30, 31.) No one else could do his job. How thrilled we should be to carry out our functions in the economy of heaven!

When Providence purposed the conversion of the Ethiopian courtier returning home from worshiping in Jerusalem, "the Spirit said unto Philip, Go near, and join thyself to this chariot." When he had completed his ministry, "the Spirit of the Lord caught away Philip." (Acts 8:26-40.) No one else could have done this task as well.

To emphasize the need for personal witness, the Spirit came as luminous and warming tongues upon each one in the upper room on the day of Pentecost. He excluded none. (Acts 2:3.) God still gives "to every man his work." (Mark 13:34; compare Matthew 25:15.) The Spirit continually flows, as oil, to each waiting heart with that special power which enables each disciple to let his own light so shine.

Jesus warned, in the parable of the wise and foolish virgins, that the individual Christian shines only by maintaining a constant supply of oil. His light is to burn with undimmed flame through the night watch. The allegiance and love for Christ, the returning Bridegroom, must motivate the life of each virgin. At first there was no apparent difference between any of them. Each seemed ready with her lamp. However, the delay in the groom's arrival exposed the fatal lack of half of them. The "foolish ones" did not have a sufficient supply of oil. All started out with oil, but only five had reserve vessels, or bowls, with enough

Oil—Luminance of God

for all emergencies. Some did not avail themselves of what had been close at hand. Those who had the oil greeted the bridegroom with shining lamps. (Matthew 25:1-13.) So must "we through the Spirit wait for the hope," the blessed hope! A lack of His presence will cause the flame to flicker and the light to go out.

"Without the Spirit of God a knowledge of His Word is of no avail. The theory of the truth, unaccompanied by the Holy Spirit, cannot quicken the soul or sanctify the heart. One may be familiar with the commands and promises of the Bible; but unless the Spirit of God sets the truth home, the character will not be transformed. Without the enlightenment of the Spirit, men will not be able to distinguish truth from error, and they will fall under the masterful temptations of Satan."—*Christ's Object Lessons*, pp. 408, 411. This quotation describes the condition of the virgins with the sputtering lamps. They lacked the essential oil—the fuel of the Spirit.

Oil needs replenishing regularly and often. Morning and evening the priest supplied new oil to the Tabernacle lamps. Likewise, morning by morning and evening by evening the High Priest in heaven must trim the lamps of the soul.

The seven-branched lampstand provided the only light in God's shrine. The oil for these lamps came from the olive: it flowed through suffering; it was beaten from the berries; it must be pure. Its finger pointed to the Holy Spirit, who came through the suffering Son. Today He pleads for you before God's throne. Furthermore, oil gives light only when it is consumed! Here, too, we read a story rich in sacrifice. The Father of lights gave His only Son as the Light of this darkened world, and He shone with the Spirit's glory. The mighty Trinity bestows on men their fullest ministry that those who will might live as stars in earth's darkest hours.

The wise virgins took oil. The choice was theirs. The carrying out of their decision was also theirs. The Spirit fills only those who eagerly accept Him. Jesus commanded His disciples, "Receive ye the Holy Ghost." (John 20:22.) Continually, habitually, receive the Spirit into your life. Luther's translation *"Nehmet hin den Heiligen Geist,"* "Take along the Holy Spirit," suggests continued companionship with Him in his journey of life.

"His lamp am I, to shine where He shall say,
   And lamps are not for sunny rooms,
   Not for the light of day;
But for dark places of the earth,
Where shame and crime and wrong have birth;
Or for the murky twilight gray
Where wandering sheep have gone astray;
Or where the light of faith grows dim
And souls are groping after Him.

"And as sometimes a flame we find,
   Clear shining through the night,
   So bright we do not see the lamp,
   But only see the light:
So may I shine—His light the flame,
That men may glorify His name."

—*Annie Johnson Flint.*

7.

OINTMENT --
Authority of God

Oil has been universally used in every age for anointing the human body. It soothes the muscles and nerves. The good Samaritan intended this when he poured oil on the wounds of the injured Jew. By counteracting the effect of sun and wind, oil helps to make the skin beautiful. Oil was also used on the hair to control it and to add luster. Christ permitted the unnamed woman in Luke 7 to anoint His feet during the banquet at the home of Simon the Pharisee. The earliest unguent employed for this task was olive oil.

Very early in the sacred record the act of anointing held important symbolic overtones. During his night at Bethel, the fugitive Jacob dreamed of a ladder connecting earth with heaven. So vividly did the vision impress Jacob that he exclaimed, "The Lord is in this place!" In the morning he set up the stone upon which he had pillowed his head as a memorial of the spot upon which the mystic ladder had rested. To consecrate this marker, the patriarch "poured oil upon the top of it." (Genesis 28:10-19.) This is the first instance of such an act recorded in the Bible.

Years later when Jacob and his family prepared to return to Canaan, Laban and his sons envied his material success and plotted to rob their own relatives. To reassure His servant, Christ again appeared to Jacob in vision and reminded him of the vow he had made at Bethel twenty years before. He assured him of the comfort of His presence. "I am the God of Bethel, where thou anointedst the pillar." Genesis 31:13. Then, He promised continued guidance and protection. The Lord regarded this pouring of oil over the stone as an act of anointing.

On a later occasion Jacob again set up a pillar. This time it was in the place where God talked with him on his return from Padan-aram, and once again he consecrated it by pouring on oil. Jacob chose for its position the very spot where he had originally dedicated himself to God. The act of anointing made the place a shrine for the Lord. (Genesis 35:9-15.)

But not until the people of Israel entered into full covenant relationship with Jehovah, pledging themselves to live as a holy nation, did anointing reveal its richest significance. This act was carried out over and over again at the inauguration of the Tabernacle. Moses anointed each part of it with oil as a sign of its infusion with the Spirit as well as its dedication to sacred purposes. He left a record of each specific object so consecrated. The Tabernacle itself was particularly mentioned, and so were the table of shewbread, the candlestick, the altar of incense, the ark, the altar of burnt offering, and the laver and its foot. (Leviticus 8:10; Exodus 40:9-11, 15; 30:26-28.)

In addition, a special service of consecration was reserved for the priests, and particularly the high priest. Their anointing set these men apart by imposing responsibilities on them which God required of no other Israelites. Aaron was first anointed, and then his sons. During the high priest's consecration he was suffused with oil. It poured from his head, down his beard, and dropped from the hem of his robes! He was thereafter designated the anointed priest. God considered his ordination final, and his duties were to end only with his death. Today the Spirit longs to anoint God's sons and daughters as His appointed priests. (Exodus 28:41; 29:7-21; 40:15; Psalm 133:2.)

When Israel demanded a king, the Lord granted their request under duress, but He stipulated that the ruler should be anointed in a solemn ceremony. This served to impress both king and people with the responsibilities of the monarchy. The procedure underlined the truth that the king's authority stemmed from a Source outside himself. The monarch ruled on behalf of God and represented His law and government. To teach this, God directed the prophet, as His representative, to perform the act of anointing. The monarchy was to rest on divine not human power and would continue as long as the Lord ordained. It would end when sin caused Him to withdraw His authorization. Today the Spirit would anoint us as His appointed "kings" and make us His "royal priesthood."

Every prophet, too, was anointed by God's directive. Men did not appoint prophets; God called them as His spokesmen to "fore" tell events as well as "forth" tell His messages. To achieve His goal, Jehovah dispatched His Plenipotentiary, the Spirit, to anoint His delegated prophets. The Lord might employ any chosen man to represent Him; for instance, Elijah received God's call to install Elisha as his successor in prophetic ministry. (1 Kings 19:16.) Today the Spirit anoints God's appointed servants to speak for Him.

From these illustrations we see that the Lord authorized these three functionaries, prophet, priest, and king, and consecrated them to their duties by a special act of anointing. They represent three vital aspects of the Saviour's mission. As God's Messiah, or Anointed One, Christ was at once Heaven's Prophet, Priest, and King on earth. Eventually, He will carry through, in their fullness and for eternity, these functions portrayed by His earthly representatives.

The Greek word *Christ* means "Anointed One" and is an exact equivalent of the Hebrew "Messiah." The oil of anointing, by which God set apart Jesus of Nazareth, was the Holy Spirit, who infused Him with measureless authority. Through every stage of His development the Holy Ghost empowered Jesus. Spirit-enlightened prophets foretold His advent. Mary conceived Him by the Holy Ghost. The Spirit prompted men to recognize in the Babe of Bethlehem the promised Messiah. Richly endowed by the Father, the Child Jesus Himself "waxed strong in the Spirit." After anointing our Lord, the heavenly Dove directed Him into the wilderness for His conflict with the adversary. There Christ gained His victory by His use of the Spirit-inspired, "It is written."

As He entered into His ministry, Jesus performed all His acts of mercy by the power of the Spirit through the agency of angels. In His sermon at Nazareth, Jesus affirmed that His anointing by the Holy Spirit fulfilled the ancient prophecy concerning the Messiah's mission of salvation. (Luke 4:17-19.) Jesus, the only Son of Adam in whom the Spirit wrought unhindered, exemplifies a completely anointed Servant of Jehovah, dedicated to His task.

The infusion of the Spirit guarantees success. Our blessed Lord vividly illustrated this by His affirmation that His efficiency and power came through the Holy Spirit. (Matthew 12:28.) Peter recognized this in his testimony concerning the Messiah. (Acts 10:38.) Christ, with all His matchless purity and profound knowledge, constantly depended upon the Holy Ghost. How much more should we, frail and fickle children of dust, rely upon His almighty power!

All righteous aspirations and actions spring from this heavenly Dynamic. The Spirit's power was not restricted to Christ's personal life only; it also reached out from Him to bless and help others. In our spheres, we, too, will benefit our associates only as the Spirit uses us.

The ointment of the Spirit sanctifies. Jehovah commanded Moses, as we have noted, to anoint particular parts of the Tabernacle and the priests. This rendered efficacious the contribution each part played in the tableau of salvation which the sanctuary depicted. Have you ever put a bag of lavender among your clothes? Every time you touched them, fragrance spread into the atmosphere. The anointing of the Spirit causes the loveliness of Christ's character to pervade all He touches. Sometimes a Christian's inconsistencies make his reputation odious, but with the ointment of the Spirit "his smell [will be] as Lebanon." (Hosea 14:6.)

The Trinity pledged themselves to achieve man's redemption. To fulfill His part in the plan of salvation through incarnation, life, death, and resurrection, Jesus "humbled himself." He served through the torture of Golgotha to ultimate triumph in glory. At His ascension, Jesus was anointed with the "oil of gladness." Enthroned at God's right hand, He is honored forever. The divine anointing made Christ King of kings and Lord of lords, and reinstated Him as Creator and Redeemer, Priest, and Potentate of the universe.

After His inauguration as our High Priest and Advocate, Christ dispatched the Spirit in boundless cataracts of grace for the blessing of sinners. Like Jesus, the Spirit humbled Himself by placing His gifts at the disposal of an oftentimes indifferent church.

The anointing of the "oil of gladness" assures us that Jesus is a Saviour with a happy heart! The joy set before Him sustained His soul in its darkest moments, and after the storm came the sunshine, and after the strife, the calm. God granted Him the "oil of joy for mourning." The Saviour shares this joy with His brethren. He has fulfilled the prophetic picture of a risen Saviour entering into fullness of joy and has overflowed gladness among His people as a blossom spills perfume wherever the wind bears it.

This anointing of the Holy Ghost is the differentiating characteristic of Christians. "The Spirit is the holy anointing oil compounded of heavenly spices and prepared by Christ for His friends."—Clement of Alexandria, *Paedagogus*, IX:85. Christians should be like Christ, that is, anointed ones. "You who have put on Christ, and been made partakers of Him are rightly called 'Christ's'; . . . there was given to you an unction which is the antitype of that wherewith Christ was anointed." Cyril of Jerusalem, *Catecheses,* XXII, Mystagogic Lecture 3. Christ is our joyful, anointed mediating Priest, and we should emulate Him.

We Christians should be underpriests, ministering the precious efficacy of the slain Lamb to meet man's need. We, too, should be kings, masters of our own hearts, leaders who recognize Spirit-filled men. We, too, in a sense, should be prophets who speak forth the words of eternal life. Ask yourself daily, How am I growing up into Christ's ideal for me?

Anointing oil touched the ear, the hand, and the foot of the leper who had been cleansed and restored to full fellowship. (Leviticus 14:15-18.) This taught that his thoughts and senses, his hearing and working, his worship and walking had thus been consecrated to God. But underneath the oil, at its very foundation, had been placed the blood of the slain lamb. Calvary undergirds Pentecost, the cross forms the foundation of our infilling by the Spirit. The cleansed and anointed leper represents humanity transformed and anointed with the Spirit.

The ointment of the Spirit heals blindness of the eye and illumines the processes of the mind. Christ continually pleads with the indifferent members of the church of Laodicea, "Anoint thine eyes with eyesalve, that thou mayest see." Revelation 3:18. The word He used here is highly suggestive; it means "to rub in," and not merely to place upon. Our Lord stresses that believers should allow the salve to penetrate. The application of the Spirit's balm must be thorough and deep. Do we allow the unction of the Spirit to reach the depths of our being so that we might observe right and wrong clearly? Many times we discern only blurred and confused images of what constitute Heaven's standards of conduct; thus we should pray, "Anointing Spirit, open mine eyes that I might see aright."

The effect of applying this heavenly ointment is described in Christ's promise, "that thou mayest see." (Revelation 3:19.) Notice that the pronoun in our Lord's statement is singular. This anointing and the resultant clearness of vision is very personal. Each must receive the Spirit for himself. Each must gain a correct view of right and wrong. And what shall we perceive as a result of this heavenly eyesalve? The Apostle Paul noted, "We see Jesus." (Hebrews 2:9.) We also discern eternal realities before unseen. We shall happily watch unto prayer. We shall carefully look to ourselves and discover our high calling. We shall also notice that the day of Christ is approaching. Let us apply the healing ointment of the Spirit to our eyes now.

The unguent of the Spirit empowers. This was the secret of the authority and success of our Lord. "God anointed Jesus of Nazareth with the Holy Ghost and [that is to say] with power." Acts 10:38. So may we gain power as His servants.

The ointment of the Spirit grants privileges. God ensured that the priest of Israel received all the perquisites of the various rituals of worship, for God had granted him no specific stipend. He depended upon the faithfulness of God's people. We are His royal priesthood today and enriched by His Spirit.

The unction of the Spirit anoints to salvation. God prepared Samuel to meet and anoint Saul, the first king of Israel: "Thou shalt anoint him to be captain, . . . that he may save my people." 1 Samuel 9:16. Jesus, the Lord's Anointed, the Captain of the host, has routed the adversary. He stands ready to free the prisoners of sin and guarantee victory for each of us today.

The unction of the Spirit fits for ministry. Of Aaron and his sons God said, "Thou . . . shalt anoint them, and consecrate them, and sanctify them, that they may minister unto me in the priest's office." Exodus 28:41. The word *minister* suggests the doing of every task, even menial ones, which may lie in the path of service. True priests always stood before the Lord. Their authorization was the name of Jehovah. "Lord, make us Thy faithful priests today," we should make our daily, continual prayer.

The ointment of the Spirit enables men to preach the gospel. It should be true of His disciples as it was of Christ that the Spirit of the Lord is upon them; because He hath anointed them to preach. Our Saviour applied this prophecy to His proclamation of freedoms promised in the year of Jubilee, which occurred after the Day of Atonement. (Isaiah 61:1-3; Leviticus 25:9-24.) Every slave was then to be freed. Today Christ stands ready to release all who desire emancipation from the thralldom of sinful habits and the bondage of death.

The anointing of the Spirit informs. "Ye have an unction from the Holy One, and ye know all things." "And ye need not that any man teach you: but as the same anointing teacheth you of all things, and is truth, and is no lie, and even as it hath taught you, ye shall abide in him." 1 John 2:20, 27. This information from our divine Teacher goes far beyond what our natural resources can attain.

Weymouth renders John's promise more vividly: "You have an anointing from the holy One and have perfect knowledge." Augustine beautifully described the effect of the Spirit in the life. "To what purpose is it that we, my brethren, teach you?" he asks, and then gives his answer. "Let us leave you to His unction. . . . The sound of our words strikes the ears, the Master is within. Do not suppose that any man learns ought from man. We can admonish by the sound of our voices. If there be not one within that shall teach, vain is the noise we make. Have ye not all heard this present discourse? And yet how many will go from this place untaught! I for my part have spoken to all, but they to whom that Unction within teacheth not, those go back untaught. The teachings of the master from without are a sort of aid or admonition. He that teacheth the hearts hath His chair in heaven." (Homily III on 1 John 2.)

What is the scope of this heaven-inspired knowledge? The Apostle John used two words for "know." One indicated a critical and intellectual discernment. The other expresses the product of personal experience. Let us consider a few areas of knowledge resulting from the Spirit's unction. "We know that we have passed from death unto life, because we love the brethren." 1 John 3:14. "We know that he abideth in us." Verse 24. "We know that we have the petitions that we desired of him." 1 John 5:15. "We know that whosoever is begotten of God sinneth not." Verse 18, R.V. "We know that, when he shall appear . . . we shall see him as he is." 1 John 3:2. No external proof is necessary for this kind of knowledge; it rests on personal experience. Yet it is the most valuable source of understanding.

The anointing of the Holy Spirit enables us to gain and retain this knowledge and to view life and its needs from the vantage point of God's eternal purposes. He also grants us insight into our immediate problems and helps us to make practical decisions. In all this knowledge the Bible is the criterion; we must check every thought and purpose by its inspired records, and finally Christ Himself is the assay house of all religious ideas. We should constantly query, Do these concepts and ideals fit in with the revelation of our Saviour's conduct and will?

The anointing of the Spirit enables us to become considerate and helpful. "God anointed Jesus of Nazareth with the Holy Ghost and [that is to say] with power: who went about doing good, and healing all that were oppressed with the devil; for God was with him." Acts 10:38. This unction brought God's presence fully into our Lord's life and from it there flowed all the power He needed. Fellowship with the Spirit produces a dynamic life of service. Christ performed incalculable good, restoring to man perfection of character in every sphere of his being, intellectual, moral, spiritual, and physical. The anointing of the Holy Spirit will enable us, as it did our Lord Himself, to be good and to do good to God's glory.

The anointed Christian may lose the blessed relationship suggested by this act of the Holy Spirit. We read with horror the story of Lucifer, the covering cherub, anointed by the Lord for his exalted mission of spreading the light of God to the universe. Despite his anointing, he fell and dragged untold millions of others to ruin. (Ezekiel 28:14-19.) The effectiveness of the unction of the Spirit remains only as long as we choose to remain true to God.

The ointment for anointing was obtained from the olive and mixed with perfume. The addition of fragrant herbs rendered the oil more beautiful, but before it might be applied it must fully meet the divine objectives. The Holy Spirit comes to do His work fragrant with all the resources of Omnipotence. He does not come with sound of martial tread and beat of drum. But quietly as a lovely perfume on the breath of dawn His presence will pervade the receptive life.

Anointing with the Spirit follows baptism, the ceremony enabling us to share symbolically in Christ's death. This unguent invigorates the body and softens the skin, rendering the person less susceptible to the scorching sun and the drying wind, and making his body more supple and lissome. Heaven's spiritual cosmetic oil renders the soul more beautiful. The Spirit takes the meaning of the baptismal ceremony and makes the new birth effective. He puts Christ into all believers.

> "Thou the anointing Spirit art,
> Who dost Thy sevenfold gifts impart;
> Anoint and cheer our soiled face
> With the abundance of Thy grace."
> —*Anonymous.*

When Mary anointed Jesus' feet with her precious perfume, "the house was filled with the odour of the ointment." (John 12:3.) The Spirit's influence cannot be confined. Concerning our Saviour-Priest the psalmist sang, "All thy garments smell of myrrh, and aloes, and cassia, out of the ivory palaces, whereby they have made thee glad." Psalm 45:8. These verses remind

OINTMENT—AUTHORITY OF GOD

us of the Lord's directive to Moses, "Take thou also unto thee principal spices, of pure myrrh, . . . sweet cinnamon, . . . sweet calamus, . . . cassia, . . . and . . . make . . . an oil of holy ointment." Exodus 30:23-25. These sweet spices, blended with olive oil to make the unguent, point to the sweetness of the character imparted by the Spirit to those whom He anoints. The authority thus delegated is not harsh or crude, but fragrant and gentle. Its influence is not brusque and loud, but delicate as a perfume, and pervasive and lingering as the breath of a flower garden. May the Spirit anoint our lives so that His spiced presence may surround us and leave the pleasure as of a lingering perfume!

8.

RAIN --
Nourisher of God

Rain, nature's richest gift to the earth, is the most criticized aspect of the weather! City folk complain about it, forgetting that farmers rejoice. When rain falls after a drought, it refreshes all nature. Workers of the soil eagerly wait for showers to soften their fields and cause their seeds to germinate. Plants spring up. Trees grow green. The baked earth, now splashed with water, dons an emerald mantle embroidered with flowers. Streams dance and sing down the hills, and fish and other animals which need water rejoice. Even birds splatter happily in the shining pools.

Rain is falling somewhere upon the earth every minute. The average thundercloud carries 100,000 tons of water, or about six trillion raindrops! (Walter J. Saucier, "Rain"; *World Book Encyclopedia*, Vol. XV, p. 123.) Let us consider the factors which produce this bountiful benison.

Vapor constantly rises from some part of the earth's surface. Trees, plants, rivers, lakes, and even the broad plains of the earth exude moisture. More than all these the vast oceans are the main sources for the formation of clouds. The heat of the sun causes thermal currents to rise. These pick up vapor through evaporation. Once this moisture-bearing air commences upward into the sky, it continues to rise until its temperature equals that of the air surrounding it. Then it stops. From an airplane we often see cloud formations spread out below like a vast ocean. God's power "causeth the vapours to ascend from the ends of the earth; he maketh lightnings with rain," the prophet recorded ages ago. (Jeremiah 10:13.)

Let us consider how clouds and rain form. As the moisture-laden air rises, it expands. This decreases its temperature. As this process continues, the air may become saturated with water vapor. Should this mass of invisible cloud suddenly cool by meeting colder air, it will reach dew point. This means that it will fill with particles of water which have condensed into minute drops, sometimes termed "water dust." We call this condition cloud or fog or mist. When further cooling takes place, these tiny droplets combine still more to form drops of different sizes. When they grow weighty enough, they fall onto the earth as rain.

Another factor in the production of rain is floating dust. Condensing vapor collects around these particles, which are generally cooler than the surrounding air, and so drops of rain form about a nucleus of dirt. The largest raindrop measures about one fourth of an inch in diameter, the smallest, about one twentieth.

Falling rain washes soot, dust, pollen, and other particles of matter out of the atmosphere, purifying the air we breathe. During the dust-bowl days of the thirties, rain often appeared orange or gray. We sometimes speak of "brown snow" when dust-laden rain has marred its whiteness. We should pray for the rain of Heaven, the Spirit, to bathe the atmosphere of our lives so that we might breathe the pure air from the mountains of Paradise!

With these facts in mind, let us seek in the stories and prophecies of the Bible the significance of rain. We shall find that it illustrates many spiritual truths, and especially does it typify the grace of the Spirit.

Jehovah has employed rain as an instrument of judgment. Early in history, the entire human race, save for one family, was destroyed by the Deluge. Desolating rain and hail plagued Egypt. During the time of Samuel, the people of God had sadly apostatized. To show them that the Lord could control the sequence of the seasons, the seer called for rain during the time of the harvest, which was not normal. As a result, the people greatly feared the Lord. (1 Samuel 12:17, 18.) In Ezekiel's prediction against Gog we find the Lord threatening "an overflowing rain" as a means of punishing him. (Ezekiel 38:22.) Christ employed rain to illustrate discipline and judgment in His parable of men who built houses either on sand or rock. The same storm struck both homes. One collapsed while the other stood the test. (Matthew 7:24-27.)

Part of the Spirit's ministry underlines the judgmental aspect of God's government. Our Lord promised that the Holy Ghost in the lives of believers would convict the world of judgment. (John 16:8, margin, 11.) God's dealing with Ananias and Sapphira underlines this truth. Ignoring the Spirit's promptings ultimately results in the sin which God cannot forgive, because the Spirit alone brings about repentance, and without His presence we do not realize our sinfulness.

Not until sin had marred the world did the Lord God cause it to rain upon the earth. The very first time it rained, Jehovah washed the world clean of all that had defiled it. Thereafter rain became essential to life! "As the plant receives the sunshine, the dew, and the rain, we are to open our hearts to the Holy Spirit." —*Christ's Object Lessons*, p. 67.

But the Scriptures contain thrilling assurances in which rain signifies blessing. "If ye walk in my statutes, and keep my commandments, and do them," Jehovah declared, "I will give you rain in due season, and the land shall yield her increase, and the trees of the field shall yield their fruit. And your threshing shall reach unto the vintage, and the vintage shall reach unto the sowing time." Leviticus 26:3-5. In the next few verses God gives seven promises: I will increase your crops, I will give peace,

I will rid you of your enemies, I will respect you, I will set My Tabernacle among you, I will walk with you, and I will be your God. These picture the Spirit's sevenfold, perfect, and complete work.

Following the Lord's disciplining of Ahab and Israel by a famine, the prophet Elijah prayed for rain. Soon there appeared a sign, a cloudy hand signaling the rain of blessing. (1 Kings 18: 41-45.) This foreshadowed the nail-pierced hands of our Saviour which reached up and unlocked the doors of heaven so that the floods of the Spirit might drench the earth with grace. Christ Himself stressed that His death, on which He based His appeal to His Father, would trigger the coming of the Holy Ghost. This took place at Pentecost, and it will happen again today when conditions are right.

All the phenomena of nature follow definite laws. For everything there is an appropriate time. Moses regarded the regularity of the seasons with satisfaction. "The Lord shall open unto thee his good treasure, the heaven to give the rain unto thy land in his season, and to bless all the work of thine hand." Deuteronomy 28:12. God gives His bounties in due season. The story of Pentecost stresses this thought. The promise of the Spirit was not fulfilled until "the day of Pentecost was fully come." (Acts 2:1.) God bestows the graces of the Spirit when we need them most.

Rain nurtures living things. The gospel prophet noted that "he planteth an ash, and the rain doth nourish it." (Isaiah 44: 14.) This word *nourish* is a rich one, meaning "to make great." It is also rendered magnified, grow, advanced, excellent, and increased. The Holy Spirit is Heaven's Agent, whose gracious ministry nourishes to perfection every aspect of Christian living.

Rain refreshes. After the sultry, dusty days of summer, all nature seems to pant in the heat! Then comes the rain. Oh, how different everything feels and looks! "In the light of the king's countenance is life; and his favour is as a cloud of the latter rain." Proverbs 16:15. This word *favor* suggests "delight in," or "to be pleased with." When the Lord encourages His children to request His loving favor, He compares His boon to a refreshing and nourishing cloud of the latter rain. Like the cloud in the wilderness, this protects God's people in all ages from the heat by welcome shade and showers the earth with its cleansing, nourishing rain. So, of course, does the work of God's Spirit in our lives.

God is not skimpy with His supplies of rain. The psalmist remarked in joy, "Thou, O God, didst send a plentiful rain, whereby thou didst confirm thine inheritance, when it was weary." Psalm 68:9. The word *plentiful* means "more than required" and applied also to Israel's "willing offering." (Exodus 35:29.) It denotes "voluntary" gifts. (Leviticus 7:16.) It designates the overflooding affection of God for His children. (Hosea 14:4.) He loves them "freely." How often the Saviour repeats this thought! He freely forgives. He freely gives the water of life to the thirsty. (Revelation 21:6.) He freely justifies the repentant. (Romans 3:24.) He bids His followers act in the same way: "Freely ye have received, freely give." Matthew 10:8. And here is one of the most thrilling promises of all! "He that spared not his own Son, but delivered him up for us all, how shall he not with him also freely give us all things?" Romans 8:32.

In Bible lands there are two main periods of rain, the former and the latter, and between these the gentle rain continues spasmodically. The early rain occurs at sowing time, between October and December. After the dry summer season, and the gathering of the last crops in early October, the ground becomes cracked and hard. The farmer finds it difficult to break up the clods for his sowing. At this juncture the early rains come to his aid. After the first showers, he can easily plow the softened soil and prepare it to receive the seed. And then, unless a gentle early rain continued to fall periodically, the seed would remain dry and dormant. So, throughout the winter months occasional showers soak the soil. The latter rain, on the other hand, falls just before the barley harvest ripens. It helps the heads of grain to swell and the fruit mature. Without its blessed ministry the earth could not yield its rich bounties.

The Bible use of rain illustrates special ministries of the Spirit under the terms "the former and the latter rain." These expressions are picturesque and significant. Early rain comes from a root which means to "cast," "throw," "plant," "sprinkle," or "wet." It also indicates "to show," or "direct," because the first showers were a sign to the farmer that his plowing should begin. In the same way, the Spirit whispers to the gospel worker, "The drought is over! The sowing time is near!"

The rain instructs the farmer as the Spirit teaches seed sowing to the Christian. God describes His rain as a "teacher of righteousness." (*Moreh* is a teacher, one who shows the way, Joel 2:23, margin.) The root of this word is the basis for the Hebrew "Torah," or written law, which is a lamp to our feet and a guide to our path. This term is expanded to include the five books of Moses. In them all God's teachings are found in shadow and type, history and prophecy. Joel's statement is most interesting. God is represented as giving "the former rain," or teacher, "with respect to righteousness." This is a prediction of the Spirit as the heavenly Teacher, whose course of instruction is righteousness.

In the purpose of Joel, the giving of the "teacher of righteousness," or "the former rain for the purpose of righteousness," has an eschatological force. While Jewish commentators saw in this prediction an allusion to the ministry of the Messiah, the main thrust of the context refers to the latter days, or the time of the loud cry. (*The Great Controversy*, p. 611.) But this is not all. The teacher of righteousness also alludes to (1) the preachers who stress the message of righteousness by faith; and (2) the message itself, for Ellen White declares, "The message of Christ's righteousness is to sound from one end of the earth to the other to prepare the way of the Lord. This is the glory of God, which closes the work of the third angel."—*Testimonies*, Vol. 6, p. 19.

Then (3) the Holy Spirit's personal ministry must be included, for "he shall teach you all things." (John 14:26.) His topics include "righteousness." (John 16:10, 8.) The same author clearly stated, "This is the only effectual teacher of divine truth. Only when the truth is accompanied to the heart by the Spirit will it quicken the conscience or transform the life."—*The Desire of Ages*, pp. 671, 672.

Another term for the early rain means "to satisfy with drink," or "to refresh with water." It pictures the thirsty ground drinking in the longed-for rain, and becoming vibrant with springing life. The Spirit alone satisfies every thirsty soul.

Still another term designates the latter rain, which fell in Palestine between March and April, and sometimes even later. It comes from a root meaning "to be late," "to glean or gather the last fruit." Two other expressions besides these apply to rain. One means a heavy rain and the other a light rain.

Let us summarize. The early rain prepared the soil for the seed's germination. Through the growing period this rain, sometimes known as winter rain, continued falling periodically. Finally, the latter rain ripened the crops for harvest. With these ideas as a background, the emblem of rain as applied to the ministry of the Holy Spirit becomes much clearer and more pointed.

As we have noted, the early rain fell in Bible lands at the time of plowing and sowing—an appropriate time, also, for the bestowal of the gift of the Spirit. He is vitally needed at the beginning of the Christian life. Ellen G. White observes, "Under the figure of the early and the latter rain, that falls in Eastern lands at seedtime and harvest, the Hebrew prophets foretold the bestowal of spiritual grace in extraordinary measure upon God's church. The outpouring of the Spirit in the days of the apostles was the beginning of the early, or former, rain, and glorious was the result. To the end of time, the presence of the Spirit is to abide with the true church."—*The Acts of the Apostles*, pp. 54, 55.

We see that the early rain is "necessary in order that the seed may germinate. Under the influence of the fertilizing showers, the tender shoot springs up."—*Testimonies to Ministers*, p. 506. The time for the special ministry of the Spirit, which Inspiration calls "the former rain," is when the soil of the heart thirsts for spiritual moisture. God promises, "I will pour water upon him that is thirsty." Isaiah 44:3. His invitation rings down through the centuries, extending to men in every age, "Ho, every one that thirsteth, come ye to the waters." Isaiah 55:1.

When the disciples waited and prayed in the upper room, they received the former rain. This sense of individual need is the prerequisite for the watering of the seed of the Word which the sower has put in the mind. The Holy Spirit will cause it to swell and germinate in the heart, bringing forth life in the soul and fruit in the experience. The part played by the Spirit in generating a new life, Scripture likens to the early rain. This ministry is absolutely vital. Everything which follows in the Christian's experience depends upon this right beginning. "Unless the former rain has fallen, there will be no life; . . . the latter rain can bring no seed to perfection."—*Testimonies to Ministers*, p. 506. In fact, "those who did not receive and appreciate the early rain will not see or understand the value of the latter rain."—*Ibid.*, p. 399.

To recapitulate, the coming of the former rain portrays the ministry of the Spirit in the initial experience in Christian living. It indicates the part which Heaven plays in starting the divine life in the soul. It brings about the new birth, or conversion, and points to the bestowal of the life of Heaven in the heart for the first time. As the former rain, the Spirit has a personal ministry for every Christian.

The former rain also marked the beginning of the Christian church. When the disciples in the upper room fulfilled the necessary conditions, Heaven responded. "The Spirit is given as a regenerating agency, to make effectual the salvation wrought by the death of our Redeemer. . . . Having brought conviction of sin, and presented before the mind the standard of righteousness, the Holy Spirit withdraws the affections from the things of this earth, and fills the soul with a desire for holiness."—*The Acts of the Apostles*, pp. 52, 53. Hosea 10:12 stresses this truth: "Sow to yourselves in righteousness, reap in mercy; break up your fallow ground: for it is time to seek the Lord, till he come and rain righteousness upon you." When the Spirit comes, He will demonstrate righteousness.

Ellen G. White continues: "It was by the confession and forsaking of sin, by earnest prayer and consecration of themselves to God, that the early disciples prepared for the outpouring of the Holy Spirit on the day of Pentecost. The same work, only in greater degree, must be done now. Then the human agent had only to ask for the blessing, and wait for the Lord to perfect the work concerning him. It is God who began the work, and He will finish His work, making man complete in Jesus Christ. But there must be no neglect of the grace represented by the former rain. Only those who are living up to the light they have will receive greater light. Unless we are daily advancing in the exemplification of the active Christian virtues, we shall not recognize the manifestations of the Holy Spirit in the latter rain. It may be falling on hearts all around us, but we shall not discern or receive it."—*Testimonies to Ministers*, p. 507.

Not only does the former rain represent the Spirit's ministry necessary for the beginning of Christian living; it is also vital for the growth of the plant which develops from the seed of the Word. "At no point in our experience can we dispense with the assistance of that which enables us to make the first start. The blessings received under the former rain are needful to us to the end. Yet these alone will not suffice. While we cherish the blessing of the early rain, we must not, on the other hand, lose sight of the fact that without the latter rain, to fill out the ears and ripen the grain, the harvest will not be ready for the sickle, and

Rain—Nourisher of God

the labor of the sower will have been in vain. Divine grace is needed at the beginning, divine grace at every step in advance, and divine grace alone can complete the work."—*Ibid.*, pp. 507, 508. This grace is the power of the Spirit, the nurturing rain of Heaven.

Every soul needs the softening, life-bringing ministry of the Spirit known as the early, or former, rain to start him off on the upward way. Without this right beginning, all succeeding Christian living will be vain. This heavenly ministry follows the drought of the summer of ignorance and sin and falls only on the dry and thirsty ground. "When we bring our hearts into unity with Christ, and our lives into harmony with His work, the Spirit that fell on the disciples on the day of Pentecost will fall on us."—Ellen G. White, *Evangelism*, pp. 697, 698.

This new-birth experience is also necessary all through the Christian's life. We must die daily to weaknesses in our lives. We must also be born again daily when we realize new areas in which we have been ignorant of our condition. The Spirit will continually bring to our view personal characteristics we need to change and will then help us to commence our climb up another rung of the ladder to maturity in Christ. Ellen White reminded, "The blessings received under the former rain are needful to us to the end."—*Testimonies to Ministers*, p. 507. This gracious ministry will be with His followers unto the end if they so desire it.

The promise of the Spirit applies as much today as it did to the disciples long ago. "The Lord did not lock the reservoir of heaven after pouring His Spirit upon the early disciples. . . . If we do not have His power, it is because of our spiritual lethargy, our indifference, our indolence. Let us come out of this formality and deadness."—Ellen G. White, in *Seventh-day Adventist Bible Commentary*, Vol. 6, p. 1055. The same writer urges, "If we do not progress, if we do not place ourselves in an attitude to receive both the former and the latter rain, we shall lose our souls, and the responsibility will lie at our own door."—*Testimonies to Ministers*, p. 508.

Besides the early rain, there was also the season for the latter rain in Palestine. "Seedtime and harvest, . . . and summer and winter" follow each other by the power of God. Each has its set time. When the grain and fruit which had germinated and developed under the power of the former rain were about to ripen, they needed more rain. Then the latter rain fell and swelled the fruit to perfection for the harvester. The spiritual latter rain, therefore, will fall just prior to the harvest, and "the harvest is the end of the world." (Matthew 13:39.)

This, as was the case with the early rain, is true in the individual Christian. There is a time when the harvest of each life should ripen. Every day souls pass into eternity, their characters formed, and their destinies fixed. Enoch, Elijah, Job, and the saints who were resurrected with Jesus and taken to heaven at His ascension, all received the ripening work of the latter rain in preparation for the reaper. They reached perfection in Christ. But the prophecies concerning the latter rain contain a specific thrust toward the very last days of earth's history. The Scriptures specifically apply the latter-day ministry of the Spirit to the remnant church, the general body of believers preparing for the coming of the Great Harvester. "As the 'former rain' was given, in the outpouring of the Holy Spirit at the opening of the gospel, to cause the upspringing of the precious seed, so the 'latter rain' will be given at its close, for the ripening of the harvest."—*The Great Controversy*, p. 611.

The Spirit aids in a maturing process. "The latter rain, ripening earth's harvest, represents the spiritual grace that prepares the church for the coming of the Son of man."—*Testimonies to Ministers*, p. 506. This must take place just before the end. "Near the close of earth's harvest, a special bestowal of spiritual grace is promised to prepare the church for the coming of the Son of man. . . . It is for this added power that Christians are to send their petitions to the Lord of the harvest 'in the time of the latter rain.' In response, 'the Lord shall make bright clouds, and give them showers of rain.' 'He will cause to come down . . . the rain, the former rain, and the latter rain.'"—*The Acts of the Apostles*, p. 55. The prophet's message to us is, "Ask ye of the Lord rain in the time of the latter rain." Zechariah 10:1. Our Father is eager to fulfill His word and to bestow His choicest Gift on us. (Luke 11:13.)

This latter rain brings about a special experience of victory for God's people. "As the members of the body of Christ approach the period of their last conflict, 'the time of Jacob's trouble,' they will grow up into Christ, and will partake largely of His Spirit. As the third message swells to a loud cry, and as great power and glory attend the closing work, the faithful people of God will partake of that glory. It is the latter rain which revives and strengthens them to pass through the time of trouble. Their faces will shine with the glory of that light which attends the third angel."—Ellen G. White, in *Seventh-day Adventist Bible Commentary*, Vol. 7, p. 984.

The latter rain may be rendered useless. Should the fruit have failed to set, or should the blight of disbelief or the insect of sin or the fungus of indifference have prevented the fruit from forming at all, the latter rain will avail nothing.

Procrastination will also render the latter rain impotent. "The third angel's message is swelling into a loud cry, and you must not feel at liberty to neglect the present duty, and still entertain the idea that at some future time you will be the recipients of great blessing, when without any effort on your part a wonderful revival will take place. . . . Today you are to have your vessel purified that it may be ready for the heavenly dew, ready for the showers of the latter rain; for the latter rain will come, and the blessing of God will fill every soul that is purified from every defilement. It is our work today to yield our souls to Christ, that we may be fitted for the time of refreshing from the presence of the Lord, fitted for the baptism of the Holy Spirit."—Ellen G. White, in *Review and Herald,* March 22, 1892.

No Christian should promise himself a future occasion for repentance. "We are not to know the definite time either for the outpouring of the Holy Spirit or for the coming of Christ. . . . Our duty is not to be looking forward to some special time for some special work to be done for us, but to go forward in our work of warning the world; for we are to be witnesses of Christ to the uttermost parts of the world."—*Ibid.* Ellen White continued this warning against postponing to some future day our preparation for the final crisis. "I have no specific time of which to speak when the outpouring of the Holy Spirit will take place—when the mighty angel will come down from heaven and unite with the third angel in closing up the work for this world; my message is that our only safety is in being ready for the heavenly refreshing, having our lamps trimmed and burning."—*Ibid.,* March 29, 1892.

Let us consider some of the factors which bring about the delay. One cause is the unripeness of the fruit of the Spirit which could be forming and maturing in the lives of all believers. "When the latter rain is poured out, the church will be clothed with power for its work; but the church as a whole will never receive this until its members shall put away from them, envy, evil-surmisings, and evil-speaking. Those who cherish these sins know not the blessed experience of love; they are not awake to the fact that the Lord is testing and proving their love for Him by the attitude they assume toward one another."—*Ibid.,* October 6, 1896.

Indifference to God's working in our behalf also restrains the latter rain. "The great outpouring of the Spirit of God, which lightens the whole earth with His glory, will not come until we have an enlightened people, that know by experience what it means to be laborers together with God. When we have entire, wholehearted consecration to the service of Christ, God will recognize the fact by an outpouring of His Spirit without measure; but this will not be while the largest portion of the church are not laborers together with God. God cannot pour out His Spirit when selfishness and self-indulgence are so manifest; when a spirit prevails that, if put into words, would express that answer of Cain —'Am I my brother's keeper?' "—Ellen G. White, *Counsels on Stewardship*, p. 52.

"The descent of the Holy Spirit upon the church is looked forward to as in the future; but it is the privilege of the church to have it now. Seek for it, pray for it, believe for it. We must have it, and Heaven is waiting to bestow it."—Ellen G. White, in *Review and Herald*, March 19, 1895, p. 178. Ellen White also gives the secret of receiving it: "The sins of Israel must go to judgment beforehand. Every sin must be confessed at the sanctuary, *then the work will move*, it must be done *now*. The latter rain is coming on those that are pure—all, then, will receive it as formerly. None receive the latter rain but those who do all they can. Christ will help us. All could be overcomers by the grace of God through the blood of Jesus. All heaven is interested in this work. Angels are interested. God can make them a host against their enemies. *Ye give up too quick. Ye let go too soon,* that arm! The arm of God is mighty. Satan works in different ways to steal the mind off from God. Victory, victory! We must have it over every wrong. A solemn sinking into God. Get ready. Set thine house in order."—*General Conference Bulletin*, 1893, p. 179.

What are the results of the infilling of the latter rain? God's people will receive power similar to Pentecost. (*Testimonies*, Vol. 8, pp. 19-21.) The Lord's messengers will proclaim the third angel's message with greater zeal. Both young and old will gain new understanding of God's claims. The last saving message will spread to all mankind. (*Christ's Object Lessons*, pp. 228-232.) The people of God will be prepared for the final momentous events and be made ready to meet Jesus.

9.

DEW --
Nurture of God

Before the entrance of sin, dew alone watered the plants on the earth. (Genesis 2:6; *Patriarchs and Prophets*, pp. 96, 97.) Today in the Holy Land and in many other countries rain may not fall for months on end, and the Lord still provides dew to keep vegetation from drying out. It is vitally necessary for all forms of life. The breezes from the sea or from the snowy mountains bring moisture over the parched land, and during the chilly hours of the night it distills. In the morning each spire of grass and thirsty leaf is laden with "the dew bead, Gem of earth and sky begotten." (George Eliot.)

In Biblical times dew was considered a most precious gift from God. Isaac prayed for it in the blessing which he invoked upon Jacob. "God give thee of the dew of heaven." (Genesis 27: 38, 39.) His son's crops, and so his very existence, hinged upon receiving this daily boon. When Moses pronounced a farewell benediction on each of the tribes encamped at the threshold of the Promised Land, the venerable lawgiver invoked this beautiful wish upon Joseph: "Blessed of the Lord be his land," and then he prayed, "for the precious things of heaven, for the dew." (Deuteronomy 33:13.) Moses not only craved the dew for the

Dew—Nuture of God

farmers of Joseph, but he foresaw God's blessing for all Israel when he said that "his heavens shall drop down dew." (Deuteronomy 33:28.)

Scriptures use dew as an emblem of the Holy Ghost. Like the dew, He comes to refresh and revive flagging life. The Spirit is ready to share His restorative power with all who will receive Him. The Christian should cherish this Gift as his most precious treasure. But too often we treat Him with indifference, or even with hostility. Yet He comes as a boon from a better land! An unknown poet wrote of these benefits:

> "Dews fall apace,
> The dews of grace,
> Upon this soul of sin;
> And have divine
> Delights to shine
> Upon the waste within."

We, too, should constantly pray:

> "Come as the dew, and sweetly bless
> This consecrated hour;
> May barrenness rejoice to own
> Thy fertilizing power."
> —*Andrew Reed.*

As the dew descends, it brings the refreshing of a higher, cooler, cleaner realm down to a world in need. Out of the thousands of promises of God in the Bible, the assurance to bestow the Spirit upon us is *"the* promise of the Father." (Luke 24:49; Acts 1:4; 2:33, 39; Galatians 3:14.) Paul wrote of Him as "that holy Spirit of promise." (Ephesians 1:13.) Like the dew, the Spirit originates in heaven. His dynamic is divine. In condescension God grants His presence to man in need. The Spirit is Christ's best gift to us.

The dew is the most gentle of all the sorts of moisture which plants receive. It never destroys. It distills so softly that it enriches even the most delicate bloom. It rests so lightly on petal and pistil that healing only results. Thus the Spirit works in the soul. He comes not to disturb, but to build. Gently and patiently He woos the heart and brings about the new birth. "In . . . the gentle dew . . . is seen the love that restores."—Ellen G. White, *Education*, p. 101.

The dew beautifies. Along each gossamer strand of the spider's web the still night hangs her diamonds. In the morning sun this insect embroidery looks like festoons of jewels on shrub and tree. Radiant spheres of moisture sparkle on the blossoms. Each spire of grass shimmers with the loveliness of light. Seeing this beauty Milton mused:

> "Stars of morning, dewdrops which the sun
> Impearls on every leaf and flower."

The Holy Spirit beautifies by His ministry. Into the night of this world He brings the glory and loveliness of heaven. Around every longing, waiting soul He spreads the beauty of holiness. And when the day dawns, and the shadows flee away, and the Sun of Righteousness pours down His cascades of light and love, then the lives of transformed souls will shine with His loveliness.

The dew invests each leaf and blade of grass with its presence. The visitor of the night catches up even the smallest seedling in its loving embrace. The dew is no respecter of plants. In this we see a picture of the Spirit's ministry. There is not a faculty of the mind nor an attribute of the character, there is not a person, be he ever so uneducated and poor, that Christ's Spirit refuses to cover with His life-giving presence. The ancient promises of refreshing reach across the centuries to us. "For so the Lord said unto me, I will take my rest, and I will consider in my dwelling place like a clear heat after rain [margin], and like a cloud of dew in the heat of harvest." Isaiah 18:4. We can see this loveliness only in the light of morning.

"A dewdrop fell from a far cloud height,
And through long hours of lonely night
The little orb with its paling light
   Was lost from view.
But earth mists soon withdrew apace,
And the great sun peering into space
Finds there his own reflected face,
And draws the dewdrop to its heaven above.

"A soul possessed of heavenly birth
Came down to do its work on earth—
What was the end of honest worth
   Who cared or knew?
But when life's hour or night was run,
The Father, seeing all 'well done,'
Finds His own Image in His Son
And takes Him to Himself in fullest love."
—Anonymous.

All this loveliness rests latently until the dawn encases each dewdrop with its radiance. Yet the dew is only water. It has no intrinsic beauty. It reflects only the brilliance of the sun. The Holy Spirit does not exhibit Himself. He reveals the splendor of the Sun of Righteousness, and through the Spirit our lives take on the beauty of Christ's character.

Scriptural imagery uses the dew to suggest acceptance. The wise man observed that "the king's . . . favour is as dew upon the grass." (Proverbs 19:12.) The word *favor* connotes satisfaction or pleasure and points to what is desirable. When the Spirit fills the life, a vast change occurs. This Hebrew word is found in other expressions, which add light to the idea of favor. The saints "delight" to do God's will. (Psalm 40:8.) The Lord's "good pleasure" is done to Zion. (Psalm 51:18.) God satisfies the expectations of all creatures. (Psalm 145:16.) As dew stimulates and vivifies, so the certainty that the King, our Father, delights in us,

His subject children, and actually desires our society for eternity, uplifts, inspires, and energizes our spirits. To think that we personally give our heavenly Father joy fulfills one of our deepest longings. The gift of the Spirit is the most precious evidence that our God wants us to be with Him.

The dew is nature's life-bringing power. "As the dew and the rain are given first to cause the seed to germinate, and then to ripen the harvest, so the Holy Spirit is given to carry forward, from one stage to another, the process of spiritual growth."—*Testimonies to Ministers*, p. 506. Plants and trees never outgrow their need of dew, and therefore God ever provides it. So the Spirit stands ready to help in every need, in every age, and in every place. With outstretched limbs all God's creation accepts the fullness of this heavenly benefit. "As the plant receives . . . the dew, . . . so are we to receive the Holy Spirit."—*Education*, p. 106.

Dew is the source of energy to drying plants. It restores vitality and enables life-forces to function again. The initial factor for the formation of the dew is the power of the sun. In Palestine the sun-drenched vapors rise from the virgin snows of Hermon till the air fills with moisture. The wings of the winds bear these invisible clouds to parched and needy places. Then in the stillness of a cold night, "the clouds drop down the dew." (Proverbs 3:20.) Upon the thirsty hills of Zion they softly distill their precious moisture to heal and vivify. All things in nature exist to benefit others. This is ever God's way. He who has gives to him who lacks. God's Spirit always comes in joyous response to human need, and when He comes, He brings a "blessing." With Herbert we ought to pray:

> "My stock lies dead, and no increase
> Doth my dull husbandry improve:
> O let Thy graces, without cease,
>   Drop from above.

> The dew doth every morning fall;
> And shall the dew outstrip Thy love?
> The dew, for which the grass cannot call,
>   Drop from above!"

The word *blessing* has a peculiar force in the Scriptures. The story of creation suggests that *bless* points to the Creator's energizing of each created thing to carry out the purposes for which He had designed it. (Genesis 1:22, 28; 2:3.) Blessing may be defined as the divine empowering to fulfill intrinsic function. The Holy Spirit carries Heaven's power into our souls and helps us to attain to life everlasting. He makes each of us into a new creation by God's grace. To receive this dynamic of the Spirit is our daily privilege for which we should constantly pray, and then "as the morning dew, His mercies and blessings will descend upon the suppliants."—Ellen G. White, *Testimony Treasures*, Vol. 3, p. 93.

The events of life obey the principle of cause and effect. Established laws regulating the sun and the wind bring moisture-filled air to the right place for the distilling of the dew. But dew forms only on chilled surfaces. During the night everything cools by radiation. Rough, tarnished, and dark objects cool first, as they are the best radiators. Was it with this thought in mind that Christ sighed, "Would thou wert cold"? Revelation 3:15.

> "Receive Him as the dew in thy heart,
>   O thirsty one, who long His grace hath sought.
>   Dew forms in stillness; struggle not nor strive.
>   What thou dost need to learn is to receive.
>
> "The air surrounding thee is full of God,
>   With love and life and blessing for thee stored.
>   Get cool and quiet, and the dew will fall—
>   A little at a time, not once for all."
>   —*Anonymous.*

Let us summarize the ideal conditions for the formation of dew. There must be a good radiating surface. The air must be still and the sky clear, for dew never condenses during a blustery night. There must be thermal insulation from other bodies, and the ground moist and suitable. When these factors combine, in the quiet stillness of the night, the dew will fall. "Today you are to have your vessel purified, that it may be ready for the heavenly dew."—*Evangelism*, p. 702.

The coming of the Holy Spirit follows similar laws. To call his attention to this, God asked Job, "Who hath begotten the drops of dew?" Job 38:28. Every birth is the result of seed sowing. Moisture-laden air currents and appropriate temperatures, interacting, produce dew. Unless all these factors balance correctly, dew will not form. Like the sun, the Father warms the earth with His cataracts of radiant love. Christ is Heaven's Agent for the expression of this love. He arises over a needy earth like the "Sun of righteousness . . . with healing in his wings." (Malachi 4:2.) The Spirit then flows from the Father to waiting hearts through the intercession of the Son.

The "dew and rain, all are under the supervision of God and yield obedience to His command. . . . God desires us to learn from nature the lesson of obedience."—*Testimonies*, Vol. 8, p. 327. When all the necessary conditions are carried out, the dew distills. For this reason Jesus advised His disciples to tarry in Jerusalem and pray in preparation for the fulfillment of His Father's promise of the Spirit. When they had obeyed His directions, the Spirit flooded their lives in richest fullness.

The dew forms where there is an appropriate place for it—a spire of grass, a leaf, a blossom in need. Dew rarely condenses on the garden paths or the hard highways of life or upon any rock or barren spot. This, too, is a parable of the coming of the Spirit. He will never fill a life which does not welcome His presence. We must first feel a need, then God is ready to meet that need. "As the plant receives the . . . dew, . . . we are to open

Dew—Nuture of God

our hearts to the Holy Spirit."—*Christ's Object Lessons*, p. 67.

The dew is found only after the setting of the sun. With the rising of the sun it disappears, thus teaching us a precious lesson. We must appropriate the blessing of the Spirit the first thing each new day. Before its heat and burden we must gather the heavenly nurture to invigorate our hearts. If we neglect these morning devotions, our goodness and strength, like Ephraim's, will vanish as "the early dew."

Montgomery has observed:

> "The dew drops in the breeze of morn,
> Trembling and sparkling on the thorn,
> Falls to the ground, escapes the eye,
> Yet mounts on sunbeams to the sky."

With the rising of the sun, the dew silently, imperceptibly evaporates. Hosea called attention to Israel's renunciation of God's goodness. "As the early dew it goeth away" (Hosea 6:4), he lamented. Today we can grieve away the Spirit. Meekness and quietness in life's relationship demonstrate His gentle presence in the heart.

The freshness of morning dew pictures the innocence and vigor of eternal youth. David looked beyond his preview of the resurrection and ascension of Christ to the day when the universe would acknowledge the Saviour as supreme Sovereign. Satisfied, he assured Christ, "Thy people shall be willing in the day of thy power, in the beauties of holiness from the womb of the morning: thou hast the dew of thy youth." Psalm 110:3. The passing years mar the beauty of youth. The flowers fade, their perfumes vanish. Life decays. But God promises that in the Spirit-filled Christian there will be the constancy of Heaven and the eternal youth of the ultimately redeemed. There need be no change for the worse in the Christian's experience; only a continuing growth toward perfection.

Of this exhilarating experience Job sang, "The dew lay all

night upon my branch. My glory was fresh in me." Job 29:19, 20. The word *fresh* may also mean "new." (Margin.) From its root come the terms "repair," as of a house (2 Chronicles 24:5); "renew," as of an agreement (1 Samuel 11:14); and "push back the encroachments of age," as in an eagle's experience (Psalm 103:5). In fact, through the Spirit we Christians may discover daily that "all things become new"! (2 Corinthians 5:17; compare Psalm 51:10, 12.) New fruit springs up in the garden of our souls. A new devotion to appreciate God warms our heart's affections. A new disposition to love our Saviour develops in our minds. We are forged, as a new and sharp instrument, by His hands for winnowing earth's harvest. A new anthem of praise sweeps heavenward because of our renewed confidence in our Lord. A new paean of adoration swells around the world because each redeemed heart shares God's victory. Ever new revelations of expanding truth enlarge the Christian's vision and deepen his capacity for devotion and service. The dew of the Lord fills our lives, and Christ pervades our hearts by His Spirit.

Dew invigorates. The life-giving power of Christ's Spirit-inspired teachings is compared with the dew. "My doctrine shall drop as the rain, my speech shall distil as the dew." The "sowing of the gospel seed will not be successful unless this seed is quickened into life by the dew of heaven."—Ellen G. White, *Gospel Workers*, p. 284. Kindness must always mark the evangelist's approach. For "as the dew and the still showers fall gently upon withering plants, so his words are to fall gently when he proclaims the truth."—*Ibid.*, p. 119. (Compare *Testimonies*, Vol. 6, p. 400; *Gospel Workers*, p. 507.)

By His Spirit God has sent inspired messages to men in every age. His words, found in the Scriptures, bring life and refreshment. He does not shout His wisdom in thunder tones. Often we hear no sound, but the Spirit speaks to us in the understood whisper of the still small voice. Let us receive His messages with eager joy.

The withholding of dew is regarded in Bible lands as a disaster. In his lament over the death of Saul and Jonathan, David cursed the hills of Gilboa with the removal of dew, because in them his friends had perished. (2 Samuel 1:21.) At the Lord's command Elijah blighted the land with the absence of dew because of the apostasy of Ahab and Jezebel. (1 Kings 17:1.) The withholding of blessing is tantamount to cursing. So when the Spirit of God withdraws from men, they are impotent to live victoriously. Only by divine aid can man think and act rightly. Every good impulse comes from God's Spirit.

The dew distills unannounced. It was this thought which prompted Hushai to advise Absalom to come upon David as silently "as the dew falleth on the ground." (2 Samuel 17:12.) The ministration of the Spirit is that of "a still small voice." (1 Kings 19:12.) His approach is without wail of trumpet or tramp of martial host. He arrives quietly.

"He deigns His influence to infuse,
Secret, refreshing as the silent dews."
—*Anonymous.*

Dew revives imperceptibly. In the burning heat of the day leaves droop, flowers wither, and grass grows seared and brown. But with the coming of the dew, life revives. The leaf is once more lifted up, the flowers freshen, and the grass is washed and green. So the Holy Ghost may refresh each of us.

"Silent Spirit, dwell with me;
I, myself, would quiet be:
Quiet as the growing blade,
That through earth its way has made:
Silently, like morning light
Putting mists and chills to flight."
—*T. T. Lynch.*

The very nature of dew causes its moisture to pervade and

saturate that upon which it lights with almost imperceptible but gentle force. The woolen fleece which Gideon left out during the night of test was soaked with moisture. You will recollect that when, on the morrow, "he wringed the dew out of the fleece," he obtained "a bowl full of water" (Judges 6:37, 38), but Gideon would never have gained this water by merely a casual touch.

We, too, must long for the infilling of the Holy Ghost. Then we will discover that God never gives His Spirit by any limited measure. But to gain this greatest of benefits, His sons and daughters have a part which they themselves must diligently play. The word describing Gideon's efforts also described the draining out of the lifeblood from the sacrificial bird (Leviticus 1:15) or the drinking of a full cup to the last drop (Ezekiel 23:33, 34). Earnestness and vigor must mark the Christian's efforts to gain refreshing from the heavenly dew. We give up too soon! Our hearts should ever be as vessels "purified, . . . ready for the heavenly dew."—*Evangelism*, p. 702. Like the widow, we must be importunate, or shameless, in our continual asking. (Luke 18:5.)

"I will be as the dew unto Israel" (Hosea 14:5), the Lord promises. Then He lists the benefits which will result. The parched and trampled corn (the King James word for all small grains like wheat, barley, and rye which have not yet formed seed) will revive and stand up. The trailing vine will flourish and spread. The lily will flower with its fragrant blooms and strike its roots deep as do the cedars of Lebanon. God's people will then fulfill all the plans He has for their development and witnessing. All this the working of the Spirit effects as divine dew.

God's purpose for His Spirit-filled sons and daughters is that they, like Israel, should be as refreshing as dew to wanderers in the deserts of sin. This plan extends to the Lord's remnant people in the last days. They are to be as "dew from the Lord" (Micah 5:7) in their ministry of healing. And when their service to others is over, they may look to a bright future.

10.

WIND --
Power of God

Movement of air is called wind. Invisible, immaterial, discerned only by its effect, the wind has ever intrigued mankind. In many lands and in many ages man has worshiped the wind. Our Lord employed wind as a symbol for the might and mystery of the ministry of the Holy Spirit. (John 3:8.) In the language of Scripture, wind indicates breath and life. The epithet "Holy Spirit" suggests the sanctifying wind of Heaven which brings life, holiness, and power.

The first time we find wind mentioned in the Sacred Story it disperses the waters of the Flood. Its forces sculptured the contours of the hills and shaped the shorelines of the oceans. The wind was invisible, but none the less mighty. At the command of God, the wind bore vast quantities of material from the ocean depths to the tops of the mountains with incredible force and in giant tidal waves. The instrument of the wind was the piled-up mass of water. Then the waters, agitated by fierce gales, more easily evaporated in the sunshine. The wind finally helped to remove the evidences of the curse.

The wind was God's instrument of defense when Israel fled from the attack of Egypt's armies. On that occasion it carved a road through the pathless sea. It piled up waters as a wall to guide the Lord's people in a safe way. (Exodus 14:21, 22.) The wind brought comfort to the Israelites, but to the Egyptians it proved a destruction. (Exodus 15:9, 10.) God's Spirit today marks out the course for us to travel in safety and joy through wayward and disturbed humanity to the very gates of Paradise.

To the fugitive David, the flying wind illustrated the speed with which God came to the help of those who cried to Him in loneliness and distress; he noted that the Lord ever sped on His journey of mercy "upon the wings of the wind." (Psalm 18:10.) Among the portents Jehovah used to illustrate His power and to strengthen the discouraged Elijah was the mighty wind which rent the mountains. (1 Kings 19:11.) This gale, coming at God's behest and ceasing at His command, revealed the wondrous control of the Almighty over the elements of nature which His hand had made.

In all these scriptures, wind portrays strength, force, or speed. With this imagery in mind, the empowering of the first disciples by the Holy Spirit was accomplished by "a rushing mighty wind." (Acts 2:2.) It blew away the last shreds of self-sufficiency and disunion from the hearts of Christ's followers. Nationalism bent before its force and surrendered its prejudices. Jewish exclusivism felt its power and stepped aside. The pressure of tradition dissipated. Then the apostles presented God's Word in all its moving power to expectant people.

The term "mighty," used of the Pentecostal wind, means violence. It suggests force which may not lightly be brushed aside. It indicates power to accomplish. The Holy Spirit bestowed upon the disciples unlimited abilities. They received power to preach with different tongues. Their authority convinced of sin, for their hearers were "pricked in their heart." They possessed unity of belief and steadfastness of purpose and so worshiped God joyously and served their fellows effectively. (Acts 2:4, 37, 42, 44, 45, 47.)

WIND—POWER OF GOD

The word *rushing* adds to this portrait of the Spirit's might. It means to carry along, or to bear everything before it. The ship in which Paul traveled to Malta was driven before the gale. Thus the Spirit impelled holy men of God to write their messages from Heaven. (2 Peter 1:21.)

The wind of God's Spirit is mighty, and His power, omnipotent. He is ready to carry all before Him to a safe haven. He will fill the sails of travel and the waves of effort so that the Christian may fulfill God's purpose for his life.

The fitful breeze may be felt for a moment and then disappear. Storm winds suddenly rise and as soon abate. Man is incapable of knowing when this will happen. So this mysterious, unpredictable quality of the wind is another fact embedded in this symbol. "The wind bloweth where it listeth," Jesus remarked to Nicodemus, "and thou hearest the sound thereof, but canst not tell whence it cometh, and whither it goeth: so is every one that is born of the Spirit." John 3:8.

Yet the wind may parch and dry and wither. It humbles and abases. When the Spirit completes His ministry, even a righteous man exclaims in disgust, "I am vile" (Job 40:4); or cries in anguish, "I am a worm" (Psalm 22:6); or protests in misery, "I am a man of unclean lips" (Isaiah 6:5); or confesses in fear, "I am carnal" (Romans 7:14); or recognizes in horror, "I am a sinful man" (Luke 5:8). The Spirit buffets that He might bless. The east wind blasted Pharaoh's corn so that the proud monarch might learn to trust an almighty Providence. (Genesis 41:6, 23, 27.) Even Daniel noted, "My comeliness was turned into corruption, and I retained no strength." Daniel 10:8.

> "He that is down need fear no fall,
> He that is low no pride:
> He that is humble ever shall
> Have God to be his Guide."
> —*Anonymous.*

Nature abhors a vacuum. Where one exists, the wind rushes in to fill it. So the Spirit stands ready to possess the cleansed soul. Call to Him to come in and abide in your empty and cleansed heart today.

Human beings cannot control the power and direction of the wind. Man must accept what comes, for the wind is independent of his will. Yet the power of the wind can change the face of the landscape! At its warm breath snow melts, birds migrate, flowers bloom, and fruit ripens. The tides rise at its whisper, and new coastlines are carved from the land at its clarion challenge. So he who is born of God's Spirit is subject to mighty, transforming forces. Touched by this invisible influence, Heaven draws the soul into a new dimension. While man cannot explain the working of the Spirit, this need not prevent him from enjoying His ministry.

Each spring the wind brings the monsoon rains across the Bay of Bengal to water the fertile plains of the rivers Ganges and Brahmaputra. Each afternoon about three thirty, the wind blows refreshingly across a knoll in Loma Linda. The wind follows regular paths governed by definitely marked thermal currents. The more man discovers about the nature of the winds, the more he learns that they obey definite laws.

We often use the expression "free as the wind," and yet Solomon long ago observed that even the apparently capricious wind traveled along regular and broad paths, "according to his circuits." He observed the laws by which they operate. "The wind goeth toward the south, and turneth about unto the north; it whirleth about continually, and the wind returneth again according to his circuits." Ecclesiastes 1:6. Nelson Glueck found remnants of Solomon's copper smelteries at the northern end of the Gulf of Aqaba. At certain times during the day the cold air from the sea rushed inland to cool the desert, throbbing in heat. Its route is confined between hills which in one place come very close together. Here the ancient engineers erected their smelter.

WIND—POWER OF GOD

A natural forced draft enabled them to reduce the copper ore mined in nearby Sinai.

Today we have discovered many of the paths by which the great currents of wind travel. The airlines are charting more and more of these "circuits." The giant planes take advantage of these natural phenomena to reach their destinations more expeditiously, for the mighty currents carry them at faster speeds. The sincere seeker for truth may similarly observe the working of the Spirit. Demonstrations of His ministry are written large in the Book of God's providences. The Holy Ghost functions according to rules discoverable in the Scriptures and also in our own experiences day by day. As we fit in with His purposes, our course to glory will be borne along by His mighty power. Although mortals cannot completely grasp the secret movements of the Spirit, yet He comes in answer to our call, and His work is perfect. Encouraged by this, we should ever pray, "Uphold me, free Spirit." (Psalm 51:12, margin.) Where God's Spirit is, He provides full Christian liberty. (2 Corinthians 3:17.)

We may easily detect the invisible wind by its effects. We hear its voice, soft as a whisper in the ripening wheat. Now high, now low, now soft, now loud, its voice rises and falls, none knowing why or when. "Like the wind, which is invisible, yet the effects of which are plainly seen and felt, is the Spirit of God in its work upon the human heart. That regenerating power, which no human eye can see, begets a new life in the soul; it creates a new being in the image of God. While the work of the Spirit is silent and imperceptible, its effects are manifest."—*Steps to Christ*, p. 57. So comes the voice of the Spirit, and he who desires to know God's will hears and understands His call. He presents His summons, and a soul is born into the kingdom of God. The work of the Spirit is clearly recognizable by its results. When there is foam at the prow, there is wind in the sail.

The wind cleanses. (Job 37:21.) The stench of humanity, the reek of animals, the exhalations of factories, and the fumes of industry would accumulate and poison all life were it not for the benign ministry of the wind. By its force it dissipates gases and odors. Rain washes the dust-laden atmosphere, and pure, fresh air comes to take the place of the foul. The ventilation of our homes is a blessing born of the wind. This purging action wonderfully illustrates the cleansing ministry of the Spirit, who drives away the miasma of suspicion and the poison clouds of criticism and gossip. He always brings into our hearts the pure, clean, shining atmosphere of heaven. With Joseph Hart we exclaim in surrender and satisfaction:

> " 'Tis Thine to cleanse the heart,
> To sanctify the soul,
> To pour fresh life through every part,
> And new-create the whole."

The New Testament writers use some interesting terms to describe the result of this cleansing ministry of the Spirit. One word means "cleansing" (2 Corinthians 7:11), "chaste" (2 Corinthians 11:2), and "pure" (Philippians 4:8). It suggests what has been cleansed, or freed from defilement, moral and physical. For instance, Paul admonished the young minister Timothy, "Keep thyself pure." (1 Timothy 5:22.) This has to do with the inner life, its thoughts and motives. Then, in outward deportment the bride, the church in its fullest meaning, must display "chaste behavior." (1 Peter 3:2, R.S.V.) In our relationships we must follow the Pattern, and be pure "even as he is pure." (1 John 3:3.)

Another word is translated "sincere" (Philippians 1:10), and "pure" (2 Peter 3:1). This betokens what has been purged of all dross and tested and found to be genuine and beyond reproach. A third term means "clean" (John 15:3) and "pure" (Revelation 21:18, 21). It is used of a "pure heart" (Matthew 5:8), a "pure conscience" (1 Timothy 3:9), a "pure religion" (James 1:27), and the "clean and white" garment of the saints (Revelation 19:8). The daily ministry of the cleansing wind of the Spirit brings about these happy conditions in our hearts, in our minds.

The wind winnows the grain and removes the chaff. In Palestine, when the harvest has been gathered in, the straw and heads of grain are ground to pieces. On a windy day this mixture is tossed into the air, and the wind carries the lighter chaff away. The grain falls into a heap and is collected. This sifting goes on all the time in the characters of each of us. In this process of separating the worthless from the valuable, the Holy Spirit plays a major role. You will remember that Jesus was "led up of the Spirit into the wilderness to be tempted of the devil." (Matthew 4:1.) We should never overlook that this rendezvous with Satan was arranged for Christ by the Spirit. He knows the time and place best suited to each case. So the Christian may gain victory over temptation and also gain insights into his own weaknesses and needs. To him who submits to this ministry of the Spirit, God promises, "I will command, and I will sift the house of Israel among all nations, like as corn is sifted in a sieve, yet shall not the least grain fall upon the earth." Amos 9:9. Eternal Spirit, winnow the chaff away, but spare my soul to serve my King.

The wind cools. Sometimes the sun beats back from the rocks and strikes at the traveler from the red sands of the desert, throbbing with the heat of the summer. The heavens appear as brass, and the land cracks. The leaves of the trees wither and fall off. The grass burns brown. The streams dry, and the thirsty creatures pant for water. Then God "causeth the vapours to ascend from the ends of the earth; he maketh lightnings for the rain; he bringeth the wind out of his treasuries" (Psalm 135:7), and the brow of the weary is cooled, and life begins again for every living thing as the water brooks again chant their songs of rejoicing. From faraway places the Spirit seeks out the thirsty soul to refresh and rejuvenate his life.

The wind fertilizes. The most universal life-spreader is the wind. Many plants cannot bear fruit on their own but await the caress of the wind with treasure in her arms. The breeze carries the pollen of a billion blossoms across field and dale. Life blends with life, fruit forms, seeds ripen, and life continues. Were it not for the wind, vast numbers of plants would perish. The petals would wilt, and the seed would not form, fertile and vibrant with life. Animals, insects, birds, and even men, unable to find food, would die. So it is with the workings of the Spirit. With an invisible caress of love, He brings the life-giving elements of another world and fills the heart with heavenly power. Through His ministry man partakes of the divine and becomes a new creation. If we would bear the fruit of the Spirit, we must submit to the heavenly "Pollinator." We should call to Him:

> "Life-giving Spirit, o'er us move.
> As on the formless deep;
> Give life and order, light and love,
> Where now is death or sleep."
> —*H. W. Baker.*

Then the peaceable fruit of righteousness will ripen in our lives.

I watched a hummingbird gathering nectar, his wings beating at tremendous speed. All his motions resulted from his own efforts. God does not use a hummingbird to illustrate the ascending Christian; He uses an eagle. Not by his own efforts, but on the wings of the wind, the eagle mounts to the heavens. Mountains and valleys bend and direct the thermal currents. The oceans and the deserts act their parts. Upon the invisible escalators of the wind the great bird soars into the blue, hardly making a movement. He merely adjusts himself to the thrust of the air currents. On the day of Pentecost the winds of the Spirit lifted the believers nearer to the celestial courts. Those who tarried to pray, yielded to His presence. The power of God came as a rushing, mighty, heavenly gale—like a tornado driving all before it, but without destruction. Today the Spirit stands ready to assist us to mount up with wings as an eagle. Let us cease our

WIND—POWER OF GOD

striving and yield ourselves to His uplifting power. We should pray:

> "Come, Holy Ghost,
>   Bear us aloft, more glad, more strong,
> On Thy celestial wing,
>   And grant us grace to look and long
> For our returning King."
>
> —*T. H. Gill.*

The wind "bloweth where it listeth." (John 3:8.) "Christ used the wind as a symbol of the Spirit of God. As the wind bloweth whither it listeth, and we cannot tell whence it cometh or whither it goeth, so it is with the Spirit of God. We do not know through whom it will be manifested. But I speak not my own words when I say that God's Spirit will pass by those who have had their day of test and opportunity, but who have not distinguished the voice of God or appreciated the movings of His Spirit."—Ellen G. White, *Selected Messages*, Book Two, pp. 15, 16. The word *listeth* comes from a root which means "to will," or "to choose." "If the Lord will" conveys the same idea. The Holy Spirit is independent of man. He chooses where to bestow His gifts. He distributes them "to every man severally as he will." "As it hath pleased him." (1 Corinthians 12:11, 18.) At Pentecost the wind came "from heaven" (Acts 2:2); then the church was born. And now the Spirit comes as God's Messenger to inaugurate "diversities of operations" (1 Corinthians 12:6) to finish the Lord's work. God stands ready to send forth His "wind out of his treasures" (Jeremiah 10:13), but He awaits our prayer for His presence and power. Make way for Him to work.

Sometimes, so ancient mariners inform us, in storms on the Mediterranean Sea, the sun and stars were hidden for days. Tossed at the mercy of the gale, the terrified seamen lost all sense of direction. In their confusion they did not know where they were or whither the hurricane drove them. Then, on the breath of the storm came a perfume, blown from the cedars of Lebanon. Overjoyed, they would know where the east lay! Their direction could be easily calculated, and their course charted. Today the Spirit wafts to us the perfume of Paradise that we might redirect our lives and plan the path to take.

In the Song of Solomon the bride prays to God to send appropriate winds that her garden might flourish. "Awake, O north wind; and come, thou south; blow upon my garden, that the spices thereof may flow out. Let my beloved come into his garden, and eat his pleasant fruits." Song of Solomon 4:16. Today the church, Christ's bride, should liken her life to a garden and pray:

> "Lord, let Thy love,
> Fresh from above,
> Soft as the south wind blow;
> Call forth its bloom,
> Wake its perfume,
> And bid its spices flow."
> —*Anonymous.*

She should long for her beloved to enter and enjoy the fragrance of the flowers and fruit. But all life would remain a desert without the winds of heaven. The north wind brings the chill of winter, killing the grubs and breaking up the sod with its million plowshares of ice. The south wind, on the other hand, bears the warmth of spring on its wings. It carries the dew and the rain, and seeds swell, buds burst, fruit ripens, and men gather a joyful and bountiful harvest.

11.

LIGHT --
Radiance of God

"And God saw the light, and it was good." However bright and dazzling light may be, however shrouded in the fog of ignorance, however despised by the conservative or reactionary, light is always good. "And God divided the light from the darkness." These two are forever apart and must ever be left distinct the one from the other. The light He called day. "Day" is when men work and walk, worship and wonder, and carry out the responsibilities of this life in preparation for the life which does not end. Light is the radiance of God in which man fulfills the purposes for his creation.

When God said, "Let there be light" (Genesis 1:3), He put omnipotence within the sphere of the world. Light is the highest manifestation of both energy and matter. When fission releases the electrons in an atom, it produces enormous power which is initially revealed as a blinding flash of light. Matter set in motion first becomes hot, then red hot, and finally incandescent. Light, then, might be likened to the effulgence of power through matter. The Scriptures employ light as an emblem for the omnipotence of God manifest in radiance.

The Bible sings of the nature of God in a three-note chord

that "God is light" (1 John 1:5), "God is love" (1 John 4:8), and "God is a Spirit" (John 4:24). Each of these epithets must apply equally to each of the Personages in the heavenly Trio. God, in His revelation of paternity, is termed "the Father of lights." (James 1:17.) Our blessed Saviour claimed, "I am the light of the world." John 8:12. Jesus affirmed the Holy Spirit to be "another" Person of the same kind as Christ Himself. (John 14:16, Greek.) The Spirit is man's Enlightener. (Ephesians 1: 17, 18.)

Light is infinitely diffusive. We look up into the sky on a clear day, and above us shines the sun. Its radiance streams through the universe for unnumbered millions of miles. At night we may gaze in wonder at many blazing suns. Their light reaches us not only across illimitable space but through uncounted aeons. Racing ever onward at 187,000 miles a second, never slackening, past galaxies of myriad suns, catching a star in its brilliance, lifting it into incandescence by the alchemy of its touch, light ever streams wider and wider in its ministry of dispelling darkness and spreading beauty. This fact illustrates the continuing work of the Holy Spirit. Is He irradiating your life with Heaven's splendor? The luminance of God springing from the Father is caught up and reflected by the Son of man. And today He diffuses this radiance through our life's experiences by the beneficent ministry of the Holy Spirit. Through Him Christ "lighteth every man that cometh into the world." (John 1:9.)

Light to discern is imparted in its genial presence. Streaming from its source, light goes out in every direction. Strike even a match, and you will see its glow from any point. The sun always shines, and shines into the uttermost. The light stemming from the sun shines everywhere, and unless an impenetrable object deliberately blocks its path, every eye in every place that chooses to look may see its brightness. It illustrates omnipresence.

Light, as a symbol of the Holy Spirit, displays many aspects of God's nature. Let us consider these in some detail. God, too,

LIGHT—RADIANCE OF GOD

is omnipresent. Sensing this, the psalmist inquired, "Whither shall I go from thy spirit? or whither shall I flee from thy presence?" Psalm 139:7. And the Lord Himself calls our attention to this truth by asking, "Am I a God at hand, saith the Lord, and not a God afar off? Can any hide himself in secret places that I shall not see him? saith the Lord. Do not I fill heaven and earth?" Jeremiah 23:23, 24. The frightened prophet Jonah vainly sought to flee from God's presence.

Like light, the Holy Spirit reaches everywhere. He crumbled the walls of degradation around Rahab, the harlot of Jericho, and transformed the heathen soul of Ruth, the rose of Moab. He found His way into the hearts of the pagan Philippian jailer and the questing Ethiopian courtier. He eventually broke into the Pharisaical mind of the proud and self-satisfied Saul of Tarsus. (Acts 9:1-6.) Today He stands ready to illuminate your heart with the fullness of Heaven's light. Do not block His entrance. If you put your little finger close enough to your eye you can shut out the light of the sun! Stop interposing your ideas between the Spirit and your heart, and God's glory will flood your soul.

Light diffuses, spreading in every direction from its source. Its luminance surrounds and pervades like a liquid. It fills everything into which it shines. Its diffusiveness illustrates still another aspect of the Spirit's ministry. He is ready to spread His presence through our lives. There is no dark cave of our minds in which sin may lurk that can long remain hidden. His light will irradiate every duty with splendor and reveal the path to glory at every darkened crossroad. His light will make radiant with His cooperative presence every task His will discerns and His providence decrees. His light will transfuse each sorrow with glory and every pain with heaven's joy. And today, as with God's love, His light falls on all, the careless and indifferent as well as the disciple and the saint. What each does with light is his own choice.

Light is essential to life. Cut off light and every living thing, plant, animal, and insect, will perish. In deep caves in the mountains electric bulbs break up the blackness of ages. Around their amber glow mosses, lichens, and even small ferns occasionally spring up and grow. The spores of these plants have remained dormant perhaps for centuries, but light called them to life. Light is the emblem of the power of the resurrection and speaks of the Holy Spirit's regenerating might. Light causes the seed of eternal life to bud and blossom and bear fruit. The luminous Spirit makes possible the development of Christlikeness in the soul. What light is to every living thing, the Holy Ghost is to every reborn Christian who longs to grow in grace. "As the plant receives the sunshine, . . . so are we to receive the Holy Spirit." —*Education*, p. 106. And how? "We are to open our hearts."— *Christ's Object Lessons*, p. 67. Throw wide the shutters of your soul, and bathe in heaven's light.

Light operates silently. Moonbeams leave no footfall. Sunshine makes no sound as it dances on the water. Yet, light's power is almost irresistible. The Spirit is quiet in His ministry. The tornado raged against the crags of Horeb and tossed the boulders into the valleys. But God's Spirit was not working thus. The lightning's fitful stabs tore the clouds apart and struck alike tall trees and mountain heads. But the Spirit's light was not thus stark or random. After the din, the silence sang clearly to Elijah's tired ear. In this stillness God was present (1 Kings 19:12, Hebrew) and might then have said, "Not by might, nor by power, but by my Spirit" (Zechariah 4:6) is My functioning. Like the light, the Spirit works in quietness and peace. Be still, and know this presence in the stillness. Pause, and you will hear His voice. Stop the rush, pull over, and meditate, and His calming words will soothe and heal.

Light brings colors into view. At night when starlight pushes back the dark, all things shade into pearly grayness. But let the moon chase the shadows with her silver beams, and brightness

Light—Radiance of God

takes the place of sable outlines. Let waking sunbeams put to flight the night, and nature decks herself in all the radiant glories of the day. Light makes color eloquent with glory. The Spirit is our light today. His presence routs the dark despair of sin and tears away the rags of wickedness and clothes souls now born anew in robes of splendor.

Light shows the path of life by which we journey up to God. David's friend Achish gave good advice when their roads separated, "As soon as ye . . . have light, depart." (1 Samuel 29:10.) This principle we should follow. Light points us to the Light—Christ. Spirit of truth, now turn us to the truth. Guide our feet along the path of salvation.

When the freed slaves of Abraham's seed set forth on their way to the Promised Land, a lambent obelisk of light guided them. (Exodus 13:21.) In spite of resentment and even open revolt, the Lamp of God led on. His illumination does not depend on man's attitude or capacity, but is ever there, waiting for recognition.

Light attracts attention. When the Spirit's light has turned our eyes from the hopelessness of our sinful hearts and weaknesses to the glorious possibilities of the path of holiness in Christ, we walk after the Spirit. His light first makes horribly vivid the foul blots caused by sin and then creates in us a new vision, a new philosophy of life, finally making *all* things new.

The Spirit points out to us the paths where duty calls in service to our fellowmen. The Spirit impelled the pious Philip to his mission field. (Acts 8:29.) The Spirit urged the wary Peter to his duty at the Roman's home. (Acts 11:12.) Today the same Spirit prompts dedicated Christians into their road of service. Where the light shines, walk! This is the only safe path. This is the highway of happiness. The journey into light will mean the most satisfying relationship with your Lord. Its goal is life in the eternal presence of Him who dwells in light to which no man will otherwise approach.

The intensity of light lessens the farther we get from its source. So the nearer we approach the center from which light streams, the more vivid will be its rays. The Holy Spirit is Heaven's Illuminator. He brings "the light of the knowledge of the glory of God" into the mind and life of the soul who desires it. But the farther man pushes away this agent of luminescence, the less light he will receive. And the more intensely he prays for the light, the more will his pathway through the mists and up the hill of Zion brighten with His presence. Why hesitate to pray for the Spirit? Why doubt? "The path of the just is as the shining light, that shineth more and more unto the perfect day." Proverbs 4:18.

Light attracts. Watch the moths, flies, and beetles at night as you turn on the porch light. Out of the darkness they come, seeking what, they know not! Look out into the valley on a dark night. If there is but one point of light, your eye will turn toward it instinctively. The Spirit proposes to exploit this characteristic of the Light He represents. As the Light of the world was lifted up to die, He became a Lamp to draw all men to Himself, and His agent to accomplish this today is His Spirit. He takes the splendor of that dying "beacon" and shines the portrait into every mind. All will be attracted save he who shuts his eyes or turns aside.

Light illuminates. When you move the object you are considering from the shadow into the sunlight, you can detect its parts and details more clearly. It does nothing to the object. It is still the same weight and the same volume. Its contours and intricacies have not altered. But everything now stands out visibly. Light therefore affects the eye of the beholder and not the object beheld. "The Spirit of God illuminates the mind of His servants." —*The Desire of Ages*, p. 354. Problems may remain the same. The play and interplay of opinions and events have not been resolved. But when the light of the Spirit quickens the mind, the details take their proper places and solution and harmony

Light—Radiance of God

result. "He gives the Holy Spirit to help in every strait, to strengthen our hope and assurance, to illuminate our minds and purify our hearts."—*Testimonies*, Vol. 6, p. 415. In speaking of the result of God's gift to the early believers, Ellen G. White observed, "Pentecost brought them the heavenly illumination." —*The Acts of the Apostles*, p. 45.

The light leads the tempest-delayed ship to its haven. In this way the Spirit beckons the sinner to the gate of the city. Thus we may be led by the Spirit. The Spirit's light will illuminate the truth and lead us to it, for "His work is to define and maintain the truth."—*The Desire of Ages*, p. 671. Those who prayed for a deeper grasp of Scripture truth "were led by the Spirit, and light shone into their once darkened understanding."—*Testimonies*, Vol. 8, p. 267. Today "the Holy Spirit is to work on human hearts, taking the things of God and showing them to men."—*Ibid.*, Vol. 9, p. 40.

Light warns of danger. The red light blinking at the intersection halts all traffic. A lightship moored by a rock is a constant boon to mariners in the darkness. By its light the helmsman turns the ship into a safe course. "The mind enlightened by the Holy Spirit may discern that it is diverging from the right way."—*Ibid.*, Vol. 8, pp. 290, 291. The Holy Spirit stands ready to convict the tender heart of sin (John 16:8, 9), but unless the Christian "yields to the convicting power of the Holy Spirit he remains in partial blindness to his sin."—*Steps to Christ*, p. 40. Let us rejoice that God "sends by the Holy Spirit messages of warning, reproof, and instruction."—*Testimonies*, Vol. 5, p. 46.

The unsullied purity of light, pointing out the defilement and dirt in the dark corners of the room, awakens the housewife to want to clean and polish! This is true of the work of the Spirit in our lives. All can be sanctified, refined, and ennobled through the work of the Holy Spirit. (See *The Acts of the Apostles*, pp. 49, 50.) God gives us "the Holy Spirit . . . to purify our hearts" (*Testimonies*, Vol. 6, p. 415), for "it is by the Spirit that the heart is made pure" (*The Desire of Ages*, p. 671).

Light kindles light. As the radiance of the Spirit illuminates our minds, He makes us lights in the world. "The spirit of man is the candle of the Lord." Proverbs 20:27. We should incorporate the luminous principles of Christ into our daily practices. This truth led Ellen White to observe:

"Every one who kindles his taper from the divine altar holds his lamp firmly. He does not use common fire upon his censer, but the holy fire, kept burning by the power of God day and night. Those who walk in the footsteps of Jesus, who will surrender their lives to His guidance and to His service, have the golden oil in their vessels with their lamps. They will never be placed in a position for which God has not made provision. The lamp of life is always trimmed by the very hand that lit it."—Ellen G. White, *My Life Today*, p. 217.

Light is the comfort of the Holy Spirit. To Israel's sons in the furnace flame of Egypt, deliverance seemed a long way off. God had long before promised emancipation, and now emancipation was at hand. The leader was even striking at their shackles. God engulfed the oppressors in the prison of impenetrable darkness, and then there shone from heaven the sword of hope. In the hovels of the Israelite camps, in the ghettos of Hebrew cities, there was "light in their dwellings." (Exodus 10:23.)

Light brings joy. The gloom of sorrow or sickness or disappointment often darkens the path of life. Everything takes on a somber hue as we walk in the shadow, cold and forlorn. Then through the word of a friend, the luminous message of a Scriptural passage, the lilt of a song, or the warmth of a prayer, the light of the Spirit breaks in upon us and changes all. Light shone at the dawning of this earth and chased away the darkness of eternal night. Light gleamed in Adam's eye as he looked up into his Creator's lovely face. When darkness wrapped proud Egypt in a paralyzing shroud, light shone in Israel's homes, and all was peace. And when the hosts of Egypt tried to strike a final blow to stay the hated slaves, light shone to comfort the saints of God and hold their foes at bay.

Later when Israel in apostasy turned from the Light, clouds enveloped all. Yet above the gloom, the Sun of Righteousness still shone, and on the fields of Bethlehem the radiance again reached this earth—the Light of life was born.

His splendor filled the shop of humble toil at Nazareth, and He still will grace all toil with light. His glory walked by dusty paths through homes made sad by sickness, leaving peace and joy instead. His shining love reached to the place of deepest sin, and there forgiveness and raptured song sprang up. His lovely light brightened the dread of Gethsemane and the death of Golgotha. The light shone on the penal isle of Patmos and spread its beams across the centuries to illuminate the last days; and from the pages of prophecy cast radiance into the face of the blackness and uncertainty of the future. And so God's people have light in their dwellings at eventide.

Light preceded the blossoming of the earth at creation, for even the teeming tribes of the ocean depths needed its beneficent ray. The cattle on a thousand hills would have perished without its genial warmth. So the Spirit's light is vitally essential today to precede the re-creation of lost souls into living beings whose lives will blend with eternity.

Our Saviour made a remarkable statement when He informed us that "the light of the body is the eye," adding, "if therefore thine eye be single, thy whole body shall be full of light." (Matthew 6:22.) This "eye" of which He speaks is the delicate conscience. (See *Seventh-day Adventist Bible Commentary*, Vol. 7, p. 965.) Only when the Spirit enlightens the conscience does it become a light to our souls. Separated from the source of light, the daily life remains full of darkness.

On the dashboard of my car I have fixed an altimeter. It tells me the height of the mountains over which I drive. However, if the barometric pressure changes, it may not indicate the correct altitude. When I suspect it of inaccuracy, I watch for a marker on the highway. When I see the "6,000 foot" altitude or other indicator, I reset the dial. Then, while the barometric pressure remains unchanged, my altimeter is perfectly accurate. This often reminds me of my personal judgment. Tossed by "winds of teachings" the value of which I may be uncertain; buffeted by the billows of mixed feelings aroused in personal contacts; beset by changing moods within my heart brought about by my alteration in health, I sometimes fail to register correct estimates of right and wrong. It is then I need the correction of the Spirit, who stands ready to guide me to truth. He is Heaven's Remembrancer. He is the eye-healing ointment. With His presence He stands prepared to irradiate my path with insight.

The Spirit-filled life of Christ's true disciple becomes Heaven's light to the area in which he lives. King David was so beloved of his followers that they regarded him as a source of inspiration and guidance. When the king grew old, his ability to take care of himself in battle lessened. On one occasion a Philistine soldier almost killed him. "But Abishai . . . succoured him, and smote the Philistine, and killed him. Then the men of David sware unto him, saying, Thou shalt go no more out with us to battle, that thou quench not the light of Israel." 2 Samuel 21:17. What praise! What responsibility!

The light of the sun is so powerful that it will fix the image of that mighty star in the eye of the beholder, excluding all else until time erases its fiery impress. This is a parable of how we Christians ought to do. Our constant gaze upon the Sun of Righteousness should burn His splendid image on our minds till He excludes all else from our gaze. Then "the things of earth will grow strangely dim/In the light of His glory and grace."

Light reflects best off an untarnished surface. How carefully we should watch and pray so that the splendor of the Light of the ages shall not be dimmed or blurred by the sin in our lives.

Light of the world, fill us with the radiance of God.

12.

FIRE --
Cleansing of God

The first time man saw fire, God Himself had kindled it. Adam had slain the initial sacrificial animal. The law stipulated that the penitent offerer should kill the victim after he had presented it to the Lord. (Leviticus 1:4, 5.) Adam laid its bleeding and dismembered body on the altar of earth, which he had erected at Jehovah's command. (Compare God's directions after the giving of the law called attention to this original altar, Exodus 20:24-26.) Adam was overwhelmed by his guilt and disgusted with himself, because he had taken the life of an innocent creature. He must have contemplated with horror the results of his action in disobeying the law of God.

Suddenly fire flashed from heaven upon the altar and reduced his offering to ashes. This showed God's acceptance of the sacrifice and death of the innocent beast as Adam's substitute. Judgment had been meted out. Thus Jehovah underlined the vital part Heaven must play in the devising and the consummation of the sacrifice. This fire made man's salvation effective. God designed that the accepting flame should bring great encouragement to Adam and Eve, for Heaven had not given them up to their lost state.

Scripture frequently uses fire as an emblem of God's very presence. "Our God is a consuming fire." Hebrews 12:29. This symbol stresses that aspect of His character which consumes what is judged unworthy of His exalted standard. (Deuteronomy 4:24.) The Lord, at important periods in history, often dramatically showed His acceptance of the sacrifices laid on His altar by reducing them to ashes with His heavenly flame. He thus gave His seal of approval to His faithful ones in different ages. Abel (Genesis 4:4), Solomon (2 Chronicles 7:1), and Elijah (1 Kings 18:38) are good examples. By devouring the sacrifice on the altar, fire demonstrated the effect of "the spirit of judgment, and [that is to say] . . . the spirit of burning." (Isaiah 4:4.) The Spirit of burning changes the old life into a new state by purging out the useless dross.

In the ritual of Israel the sinner regarded the offering as his substitute. It stood in the place of the guilty one who should have perished for his iniquity. To illustrate this principle of vicarious sacrifice, the animal was slaughtered in the penitent's stead by the penitent's own hand and then reduced to ashes on the altar. Hence, all who sense their guilt and yet aspire to holiness, cry, "Who among us shall dwell with the devouring fire?" Isaiah 33:14. Immediately the answer comes from the throne, "He that walketh righteously." Verse 15. Only those individuals whom Heaven regards as blameless will remain unconsumed in the judgment, for God rejects the rebellious and useless, and will "burn up the chaff with unquenchable fire." (Matthew 3:12.) Satan has ever tried to get men to believe the very opposite —that the wicked will dwell in the everlasting flames of hell forever! But the Bible teaches that these incorrigible sinners will be completely burned up. The righteous alone will remain unscathed by the final fiery judgments of our great God. The Spirit of burning vindicates those whom Heaven approves.

The divine flame, we have noted, consumes the sacrifice on the altar. By this token it also validates the character of the righ-

FIRE—CLEANSING OF GOD

teous. The flaming desert bush illustrated this truth. Moses observed that it remained unconsumed by the fire which engulfed it and sought to destroy it. In this enacted parable, wood defied its destroyer! It held at bay its greatest adversary, the flame. Here was a portrayal of the incarnation. This phenomenon of the burning bush pointed forward to the glorious and heartening truth that one day Jehovah would take full possession of a human body. Because of His sinlessness, Mary's Son, and God's, did not perish. Divinity and humanity perfectly blended in Him. Notwithstanding this, sinful flesh wherever found would ever burn up. In Christ's human body Heaven's flame, the Holy Spirit, found a safe home. God wishes that we, too, should be filled with His fiery Spirit. His divine presence will not destroy, but only purge and exalt our surrendered natures into luminous glory. The Spirit is Heaven's great Approver.

God's fire, therefore, consumes only what God decides is unacceptable. The heavenly Judge carefully considered the fate of Sodom and Gomorrah. Because He estimated them to be unchangeably reprobate, the inhabitants of these cities were finally immolated by Jehovah's judgments. Another illustration of the judicial action of fire is the case of the first anointed priests. "Aaron's sons took the common fire which God did not accept, and they offered insult to the infinite God by presenting this strange fire before Him. God consumed them by fire for their positive disregard of His express directions. All their works were as the offering of Cain. There was no divine Saviour represented."—Ellen G. White, *Redemption*, No. 2, pp. 82, 83. On a later occasion fire struck from heaven and burned up the 250 princes who had revolted against Moses. When His will was deliberately and finally resisted, as in the instance of Ananias and Sapphira, the judgment of God's Holy Spirit cut down the guilty ones.

The dust of pride, the rags of self-righteousness, the fig leaves of pretension, the blooms of infidelity, the chaff of doubt, the stubble of human effort, the brambles of criticism, the filth of lust, all these the Spirit's presence will purge away. He is the Spirit of burning. In autumn, the air is redolent of burning russet leaves and useless limbs, but after the cold of winter, fire's genial heat brings life to the leafless limbs and makes the seemingly barren blossom with fragrant flowers which mature to luscious fruit. The hot iron takes away the creases in the garments of life without destroying them. So the Spirit is the Lord's cleaning agent. His mercy spares the valuable and invests the potential with life.

Thus fire tests and purifies by burning out the dross. When the goldsmith turns the flame onto the metal, he wishes to destroy the dross which dulls its luster and impoverishes its value. He blows the heat into the very heart of the ore so that the pure gold or silver may emerge, gleaming and beautiful, ready to flow into whatever mold the master artist designs. The liquid gold and dull rubbish have parted. The fire has vanquished the earthy and charmed the precious and purified it into the light. So will the Spirit subdue and purify. Jesus likens Himself to a refiner of precious metals. (Malachi 3:2-6.) By the purging flame of His Spirit He seeks to enable the pure gold of faith and love or the silver of obedience to appear in all their preciousness and beauty. "Let the heart melt into tenderness before God, as we recall His merciful dealings with us. Let the Spirit of God, like a holy flame, burn away the rubbish that is piled up at the door of the heart, and let Jesus in; then His love will flow out to others through us, in tender words and thoughts and acts."—*Testimonies*, Vol. 5, p. 490.

There are two words in the New Testament rendered "purify." One points to what has been washed, as by water. It is found in our name Katherine. The other (1 John 3:3) speaks of a burning process that consumes the evil with which it comes into contact. With the Christian hope shining in his heart, dependent completely upon God, surrendered to the control of His

Fire—Cleansing of God

Spirit, man "purifieth himself, even as he is pure." (1 John 3:2, 3. Here the middle voice is used; the person has a work to do for himself.) We constantly should pray:

> "Refining fire, go through my heart,
> Illuminate my soul;
> Scatter thy life through every part,
> And sanctify the whole."
> —*Charles Wesley.*

Fire cleanses. The Lord gave specific directions to His people. He declared, "Every thing that may abide the fire, ye shall make it go through the fire, and it shall be clean." Numbers 31:23.

> "For the common wooden vessel
> 'Tis enough it should
> Simply have the water cleansing,
> It is only wood;
> But for vessels, costly, golden,
> Used for service higher,
> They are only made the brighter,
> Passing through the fire.
>
> "Am I tempted in the furnace
> From my heart to cry,
> 'Stay Thine hand! Oh 'tis enough, Lord!
> Still the agony'?
> Till Thine image is reflected
> In the burnished gold,
> Lord, I ask that Thou wilt grant me
> Patience manifold."
> —*Anonymous.*

The presence of the Holy Spirit in our lives renders us holy by His sanctifying touch.

The Baptist prophesied that one phase of Christ's ministry

for fallen men would be carried out by the purifying, warming presence of the Holy Spirit. "I indeed baptize you with water," he proclaimed to the people, "but he [the Messiah] . . . shall baptize you with the Holy Ghost, and with fire." (Matthew 3:11. The "and" is an epexegetical particle and makes "fire" explain what has just been mentioned. It may be rendered "*viz.*" or "that is to say.") The evangelist here stressed that Christ's baptism in the heavenly fire was actually a baptism of the Holy Ghost.

Our Lord endorsed the Baptist's word by His one promise to send fire upon earth to separate the valuable from the useless. "I am come to send fire on the earth; and what will I, if it be already kindled?" Luke 12:49. This is not literal fire, of course. But, like fire, the Spirit's presence cleanses, warms, illuminates, and kindles. Christ's prediction and prayer were fulfilled on the day of Pentecost, when cataracts of the heavenly Presence cascaded upon the waiting believers. The symbol which the Spirit chose, as an illustration of this function of His ministry, was, of course, fire in the shape of cloven tongues. (Acts 2:1-4.)

The Baptist, as we have noted, contrasted his own mode of baptism in water with his Lord's baptism in fire. We should observe that both symbols, water and fire, illustrate different means of cleansing. The purification effected by water is ephemeral and superficial; that produced by fire is permanent and deep. Water leaves man's body cleansed of external defilements. It must be repeated over and over again. Fire, however, destroys the useless dross once and for all and exposes the shining silver of perfect obedience.

It is interesting to remember that Jesus actually baptized no one in water! (John 4:2.) When our Saviour fulfilled the Baptist's prediction, the Spirit engulfed His disciples in the upper room. The emblem of this act was the presence of Heaven's Flame resting on each. Fire gave visibility to their new relationship, and power marked their works of conversion and proclamation. Baptism by water was administered by the servant, but baptism by fire the Master administered. Baptism by water was the outer symbol; baptism by fire, the inner dynamic. One covered the body, the other penetrated the thoughts and intents of the heart.

What is the significance of baptism in fire? The word *baptize* means to plunge, to bury, to submerge, and underlines the thought of unresisting committal. The candidate is "dead." He surrenders himself to the element of water and sinks into it. John the Baptist, by this word, illustrated the measure of the complete covering, submerging, and burying of the Christian in the Holy Spirit.

The penitent must yield his life and ways to the Spirit by several simple steps. Before baptism, the candidate must repent of his sins and change his mode of thought. This requires the total surrender of his will to God. The young Christian must thirst for the waters of the Spirit. (John 7:37-39.) He must implore the Lord for the infilling of the Holy Ghost. (Luke 11:9, 13.) He must believe that God will send the Comforter as his life's companion. Then the penitent must consider himself dead to his past life and allow the Spirit to take over complete control of his future. By his decision he moves from one element in which he has lived to another. By faith he is now in the fire of God's presence, and in this new sphere he purposes to live. Christ's personal Representative saturates man's coldness with the ardor of divine love, immersing him in the Holy Spirit!

Paul records that God uses fire to expose the true worth of every man's lifework. (1 Corinthians 3:13.) Whatever part of human achievement resists and survives the fiery trials, which day by day test the soul, will endure forever. The apostle compares God's day of final accounting with the application of fire which consumes what is combustible and leaves the hidden treasure unimpaired. (1 Corinthians 3:10-15.) What the fire approves, it therefore vindicates. Paul observed encouragingly that although the final flame may destroy the worthless superstructure of human endeavors, it is possible for the careless builder to escape with his life, but with little else. Fire thus symbolizes the searching yet merciful action of God's holiness carried out by the Spirit.

> "O Fire of God, burn on, burn on,
> Till all my dross is burned away;
> O Fire of God, burn on, burn on.
> Prepare me for Thy testing day."
> —*Anonymous.*

Our Saviour used an interesting illustration of this truth, which He took from the religious ritual of Israel. "Every one shall be salted with fire," He noted, then He added, "[that is to say,] . . . every sacrifice shall be salted with salt." (Mark 9:49; compare Leviticus 2:13.) Ellen White comments on these words thus: "No sacrifice would be acceptable to God which was not salted or seasoned with divine fire, which represented the communication between God and man that was opened through Jesus Christ alone."—*Redemption*, No. 2, p. 82. Salt seasons and preserves. No decay-bringing bacteria can grow where it is found. So is he who, as a living sacrifice, is seasoned with the preserving, flavoring presence of the Holy Spirit. When the heavenly Flame comes into the surrendered life at Christ's behest, the right and the wrong each takes its separate place in the thinking of the Christian. By the fire of the Spirit, Heaven communicates with those whom God longs to purify.

Fire as used in cooking makes food fragrant and palatable. So the fiery Spirit transforms the sacrifice of our lives, "the food of the offering" (Leviticus 3:11, 16), into a sweet-smelling savor, acceptable and pleasing to God.

At the Feast of Pentecost, or the Feast of the Holy Spirit, Israel presented two loaves to the Lord. They point to both the Jew and the Gentile whom Heaven regarded alike. When united in the Christian church, they were to be living sacrifices to God.

These loaves, unlike other meal offerings, were baked with leaven. Scripture often uses leaven as a type of the pervasive working of sin and selfishness. But through the baking process, fire kills leaven and makes the loaves acceptable to God. (Leviticus 23:17.) When we present our lives to the mighty working of the Spirit, He will destroy all the insidious influences of the leaven of unrighteousness and render us acceptable to God.

Fire guides God's elect. The pillar of fire blessed the Lord's ancient people during the darkness. Through it "God communicated with Israel, revealing to men His will, and imparting to them His grace. God's glory was subdued, and His majesty veiled, that the weak vision of finite men might behold it."—*The Desire of Ages*, p. 23. The light of a fire is not dazzling. Often we sit watching the dancing flames on the logs in our fireplaces, and in their light we discern soft beauty and subdued joy. The Spirit is God's gentle Illuminator, revealing to us changing and thrilling visions of eternal glory.

The children of Israel were led into the wilderness of test and trial by the pillar of fire. Jesus was actually led by the Spirit into the wilderness to be tempted by the devil! (Matthew 4:1.) The divine Leader guided the Son of God to the flaming crucible, where His character was tried as Israel's had been long before. The Apostle Peter encourages us today not to allow ourselves to be disturbed by fiery trials (1 Peter 4:12) which may test our souls. When the process is over, he assures us, our characters will come forth pure and strong. The divine encouragement is still true, "When thou passest through the . . . fire, thou shalt not be burned; neither shall the flame kindle upon thee." Isaiah 43:2. Never forget that the fire, lighted by the Spirit, did not consume the bush in the desert, nor will it destroy the soul baptized into Christ and led by the Spirit for assaying. The Spirit purifies only that we might pass all tests.

Fire kindles lamps. Its luminiferous ray gives light. From the smallest flame, the most brilliant lamp may take its beginning.

(See James 3:5.) So the Holy Spirit's lambent presence in the surrendered soul makes the entire life glow with heavenly glory. He lightens the conscience and gives insight to the believer. He illuminates the intellect. He leads the mind into the fullness of truth. (John 16:13.) He opens the spiritual vision to otherwise inscrutable attainments in the daily experience. The Spirit kindles the affections of the regenerate heart. The thoughts glow with the fire of true idealism. By His presence the messages of God may be read more clearly. Ellen White promised, "The Holy Spirit, shining upon the sacred page, will open our understanding, that we may know what is truth."—*Testimonies to Ministers*, p. 112.

Fire subdues. It melts the wax so that it may take perfectly the impress of the seal. It tames the hardest steel, reducing it to a docile stream which can flow into any mold and shape into any form. There is nothing too hard or too tough for fire to conquer. The most sinful heart feels the softening love of the Holy Ghost and, if it is willing, may be vanquished by Him. "It is by the Spirit of truth, working through the Word of God, that Christ subdues His chosen people Himself."—*The Desire of Ages*, p. 671. (Compare *Prophets and Kings*, p. 425, where the way of hardening is explained.) When the Spirit's appeals are resisted, the human heart hardens. However, the Lord knows our thoughts and purposes, and how easily He can melt us if we submit! His Spirit, like a fire, stands ready to subdue even our flinty hearts. He can awaken in our souls the blaze of enthusiastic love and tenderness. He can generously decant upon us every grace of His holiness and set aflame our cold self-regard and make us fervent ministers of self-forgetting devotion.

Fire makes permanent. Its heat melts the enamel on the vase. When the glazing is burnt on the pottery, the colors become permanent. So the Holy Ghost settles and establishes our dispositions. The child of God, rooted and grounded in the Spirit, will remain steadfast and unshakable when confronted by every kind

Fire—Cleansing of God

of test and affliction. With Paul we may say, "None of these things move me" (Acts 20:24), when the Spirit gives us this divine steadfastness.

Fire fuses metals. The fire's uniting flame can weld separate pieces of steel. When the unrecognized Saviour talked with the discouraged disciples on their way to Emmaus, they later recalled, "Did not our heart burn within us?" Luke 24:32. They spoke of *heart* in the singular! The Spirit's warming presence unites believers of all races and colors. In the melting pot of the church, the fire of God will make all men one in His love. (John 17:21.) The kindling Spirit's work with us blends all in the unity of faith, perfection, and love in Christ. The Spirit brings accord and cooperation in affection and service.

Fire frees. Only the ropes which bound Shadrach, Meshach, and Abednego were affected by the flames when these men were flung into the fiery furnace. Thousands of Satan's captives were released through the sermons of Peter, which touched their bonds with the celestial torch lighted by the fire of Pentecost. The Spirit never restricts the Christian's actions. He emancipates! His presence frees the prisoners of hope and sends them on life's voyage to Paradise unafraid.

Fire energizes. The prophet Jeremiah felt this inner dynamic compelling him to action, like steam pent up within the cylinder. "His word was in mine heart as a burning fire shut up in my bones," he affirmed, "and I was weary with forbearing, and I could not stay." Jeremiah 20:9. The fire in the plane's jet engines, in the automobile's motor, in the ship's turbines drives these crafts across the pathless ways to their havens. The Holy Spirit empowers us with His divine energy and fires all the dynamics of our lives into Christian action.

The fire of the Spirit added fervor to the words of moving eloquence spoken by the apostles on the day of Pentecost. The tongue of fire "was an emblem of the gift then bestowed on the disciples, which enabled them to speak with fluency languages with which they had heretofore been unacquainted. The appearance of fire signified the fervent zeal with which the apostles would labor, and the power that would attend their works." —*The Acts of the Apostles*, p. 39. An Old Testament occurrence had paralleled this New Testament experience. "The live coal of pardon" (Ellen G. White, *Counsels to Teachers*, p. 370) from the altar of the Temple in Jerusalem rendered the prophet Isaiah's lips clean. This "live coal is symbolical of purification, and it also represents the potency of the efforts of God's true servants."—*Gospel Workers*, p. 23. It made warmly eloquent Isaiah's preaching of the great gospel message for his own day. His warm words reach down the centuries to kindle our cold hearts. Of God's New Testament servants Ellen White remarks, "With what burning language they clothed their ideas as they bore witness for Him! . . . The Spirit animated them and spoke through them."—*The Acts of the Apostles*, p. 46. If the live coal "touches the lips, no impure word will fall from them." (Ellen G. White, in *Seventh-day Adventist Bible Commentary*, Vol. 4, p. 1141.) May this be the case with our witnessing too, as God's fiery Spirit cleanses and warms our lips today.

Fire spreads. I have watched it speed across the prairie and leap from tree to tree in the forest. When at Pentecost the Holy Spirit took possession of His human witnesses, the love of God and His message quickly enlarged their sphere of influence from Jerusalem to Judea. Thence they moved to Samaria and finally embraced the uttermost parts of the earth. (Acts 1:8.) This result could never have been achieved by man's effort alone. "God has provided divine assistance for all the emergencies to which our human resources are unequal. He gives the Holy Spirit to help in every strait, to strengthen our hope and assurance, to illuminate our minds and purify our hearts. He provides opportunities and opens channels of working. If His people are watching the indications of His providence, and are ready to cooperate with Him, they will see mighty results."—Ellen G. White, *Prophets and*

Kings, p. 660. Our longing cry should be, "Fiery Spirit, spread Thy flame abroad through us with speed!"

Fire warms and cheers the wet and cold! When Jesus met the disciples after the fruitless night and the miraculous catch of fish, He had a fire of coals as well as a breakfast waiting for them. Our Saviour provided warmth and food. These items illustrated the Spirit and the Bread of life. The infrared rays of the flame cause this heating effect. The Spirit transforms the coldness of our formalism and mechanical witnessing by His warming radiance. Some of us Christians give only a cold light, like a firefly! But mere light is not enough. We also need the warmth of God's Spirit in our witnessing. As our lives touch the experience of others, the warmth of the Spirit in our hearts will enliven and enhearten them. He kindles the heart, or the affections, into a divine radiance. Old things pass away. Selfishness dies. Our influence will then glow with His affection.

Fire protects. In primitive areas when settlers first moved in, they often set fires in a circle to keep wild animals at bay. Within the surrounding flames they were safe. The fire of God held the Egyptian army at bay and enabled the hosts of Israel to escape across the Red Sea. Ellen White observed that "the gift of His Holy Spirit, rich, full, and abundant, is to be to His church as an encompassing wall of fire, which the powers of hell shall not prevail against."—*Testimonies to Ministers*, p. 18. It is the way of wisdom to remain within this sheltering screen. To stray from the Spirit's protection means to perish eternally.

Centuries ago Israel made its choice. The flames started by an unknown Roman's torch destroyed their treasured Temple and reduced their proud city to ashes. That fulfilled half the prediction. The Spirit of judgment consumed the unpenitent. The other half of the promise was fulfilled at Pentecost when the holy flames, lighted by the Saviour-Priest from Heaven's highest altar, filled the heralds of God's evangel with glowing energy and impelled them to move out into the world to seek and save the lost. In every age men and nations make their choice, and we must make ours too. "The fire shall try every man's work of what sort it is." 1 Corinthians 3:13. Are we building into our characters gold, silver, and precious stones, or wood, hay, and stubble? (Verse 12.) "Our God is a consuming fire." Our choice decides whether like straw we shall writhe in the flame for a moment and perish, or like gold or precious stones sparkle and gleam with glory forever. The choice is ours.

> Celestial Fire, burn in me,
> So will my mind ever cleansed be.
> May I, my dross, my sin, myself,
> Consumed and purged, be like Thyself.
> Burn then in me.
>
> Celestial Fire, glow in me,
> So will my heart become hot for Thee.
> May I, my powers, my talents warmed,
> With love for Thee and souls be formed.
> Glow then in me.
>
> Celestial Fire, shine in me,
> So will my life incandescent be,
> May I, my lips and face aglow,
> All Thy light and joy now show.
> Shine then in me.

13.

HAND --
Fellowship of God

The hand is the most marvelous instrument ever devised! We can develop it to lift a hundred times its weight, or train it to detect even one thousandth of an inch. All man's arts and sciences depend on manual dexterity. The wonder and usefulness of the human hand unmistakably point to the skilled Designer who fashioned this tool for the blessing of humanity and the glory of God.

Next to his face and tongue, the hand expresses a person's feelings most vividly. He gestures to emphasize his meaning, and he may use signs to convey force to his purposes. The hand points out the way and stops progress! It steadies and impels. It disciplines and encourages. The hand symbolizes many ideas and activities. Because of its unique effectiveness the Bible employs the hand to depict several aspects of the Holy Spirit's ministration.

The hand of God illustrates the Spirit's affiliation with His prophets. On one occasion "the hand of the Lord was strong" upon Ezekiel. (Ezekiel 3:14.) At another time a being as bright as fire "put forth the form of an hand." The prophet explained the meaning of this gesture in the words, "The Spirit lifted me up." (Ezekiel 8:1-3.) On his initial call to the prophetic office, Ezekiel notes, "An hand was sent unto me; and, lo, a roll of a book was therein." Ezekiel 2:9. God bade the prophet to devour the teachings of this handwritten scroll. Having digested its contents, Ezekiel was to go forth and preach its message uncompromisingly. The hand of God suggests the Spirit's strengthening authority. "The Spirit took [him] . . . up," and "the hand of the Lord was strong" upon him. (Ezekiel 3:1-4, 12-14.) This imposition of the hand of God infused the prophet with the Spirit. God repeated this empowering by His indwelling presence during later crises in Ezekiel's life. (Ezekiel 37:1; 40:1, 2.) Being in God's hands means being in touch with His power.

The hand of God represents the ministry of the Spirit as Heaven's Instructor. (See Job 27:11.) The Holy Ghost was the prophet's Teacher, and today He brings to our knowledge all we need to know. (John 14:26.) Our Saviour has authorized Him to teach us the ways of life. The Christian is under the custody and power of Christ when he is in the hand of God.

Jeremiah's call had proceeded along similar lines to that of Ezekiel. To encourage the reticent youth, and to draw him into an enriching divine fellowship, "the Lord put forth his hand, and touched" Jeremiah's lips. By this act, Jehovah assured the prophet of assistance in service beyond his own abilities. "I have put my words in thy mouth," He affirmed. (Jeremiah 1:9.) Like Ezekiel, God enabled Jeremiah to say, "Thy words were found, and I did eat them; and thy word was unto me the joy and rejoicing of mine heart: for I am called by thy name, O Lord God of hosts." Jeremiah 15:16.

Centuries before Jeremiah's time, Elijah had been mightily strengthened by the touch of the divine hand. (1 Kings 18:46.) After his ordeal at Carmel, the Spirit's power sustained the weary prophet. He was invigorated to run ahead of the chariot of Ahab for some twenty miles from Carmel to the royal city of Samaria.

Hand—Fellowship of God

In similar fashion, the hand of the Lord later empowered John to fulfill his lonely Patmos ministry. Through the enlightening Spirit, the beloved apostle, now aged, was drawn into a deeper fellowship of understanding with Christ and was thereby inspired to write the Book of Revelation. (Revelation 1:17.) No man is so weak in knowledge or lacking in strength but that the Holy Spirit can endue him with adequate power to fulfill the divine program in his life.

The hand of God represents the Spirit's support and protection of His chosen instruments. When John the Baptist was a child, the people marveled at him. They recorded in awe that "the hand of the Lord was with him." (Luke 1:66.) The Father does not leave us lonely orphans. The gospel poet-prophet expresses the trust of the redeemed in God's fellowship with this ringing affirmation: "In the shadow of his hand hath he hid me." Isaiah 49:2. By the same assuring figure God promises each of His children, "I have covered thee in the shadow of mine hand." Isaiah 51:16. We have often watched a child run to his mother for fear of a barking dog. Her hand laid on his head banishes his terror and brings a sense of protection. Similarly, the Spirit ever spreads a shelter over His loving, trusting children today.

You will recall the story of the dying Jacob. As he felt his end near, he called his sons and their families about his bed. There he predicted future developments in their lives based on his knowledge of their characters. When he came to Joseph, he remembered the struggles through which he had passed. He noted with satisfaction the help which God had given him at each crisis in his life. Then he observed, "His hands were made strong by the hands of the mighty God of Jacob." Genesis 49:24. When we were learning to write, the teacher would occasionally place her hand over ours and guide the pencil in the formation of the letters. Remember, the less we struggled, the better were the finished characters. Joseph had submitted to his Lord. His Spirit's strengthening hand had enabled the young man to surmount his obstacles and attain an eminence which none of his brothers ever reached. The guiding hand, Jacob noted, is that of a tender shepherd as well as a firm foundation—the Rock of Ages.

By the time David came to lay down his scepter, he sensed a profound truth. "In thine hand is power and might; and in thine hand it is to make great, and to give strength unto all," he sang. (1 Chronicles 29:12.) His talents, he realized, were trusts from the Lord. "All this store that we have prepared to build thee an house for thine holy name cometh of thine hand, and is all thine own." 1 Chronicles 29:16. In times of trouble, Isaiah predicted, "the hand of the Lord" will be laid upon His servants to comfort and aid. (Isaiah 66:13, 14.) God promises the fearful in every age, "I the Lord . . . will hold thine hand, and will keep thee." Isaiah 42:6. Our part is to trust.

By his hand man points the way. The hand of God pictures the Spirit's guidance. As a result of his many experiences, the psalmist exulted, "My times are in thy hand." Psalm 31:15. He sensed God's directing presence on all occasions. He knew that whatever might be his quandary, "even there shall thy hand lead me, and thy right hand shall hold me" in closest fellowship. (Psalm 139:5-10.) This lesson of trust he passed on to Solomon. "The king's heart is in the hand of the Lord," he testified to the young man, and added, "He turneth it whithersoever he will." Proverbs 21:1. It was a pity that Solomon did not always heed this advice. The Holy Spirit is ready to direct the ways of God's yielded children today. Let us constantly strive to keep our hearts under the guidance of His hand.

The Lord does not lead individuals only. He is also in complete charge of the larger affairs of mankind. Ezekiel viewed the "complicated play of human events" represented by the wheels within wheels. (See Ezekiel 1 and *Education*, p. 178.) He noted with satisfaction that the form of a hand guided and controlled this seemingly confusing machinery. The affairs of nations, he observed, ultimately progressed along the lines by which the Holy Spirit directed them. The Spirit of God had guided to a successful climax Heaven's purposes during the creation of this world. Today Heaven's counsels are realized by His directing hand. (Acts 4:28, 30.) The Holy Spirit is Heaven's superintendent of all God's plans for us.

The sign language of the Hebrews applies many other uses of the hand to the activities of the Holy Spirit. David noted that God's gracious provisions to feed His myriad creatures come from His open hand. (Psalm 104:28.) The skilled hands of the craftsman illustrate the Lord's ability to carry out His many designs. Christ Himself assured His followers that His power to defend His children and preserve His chosen ones rested in His divine hand! (John 10:28, 29.)

To wash one's hands affirmed one's innocence. The origin of this act is shrouded in the mists of the long past. If a corpse was found near a village, the ancient Hebrew law given to Moses decreed that the elders should assume responsibility for the suspected murder. A heifer was then sacrificed as a sin offering in expiation. The priests were to superintend the elders as they washed their hands over the heifer while they declared their innocence. (Deuteronomy 21:1-9.) Was it of this ceremony that David sang, "I will wash my hands in innocency; so will I compass thine altar, O Lord"? (Psalm 26:6-10.) Pilate partially carried out this ritual of the Hebrews at the trial of Jesus, thus protesting his guiltlessness at the murder of the Man of Nazareth. Little did the governor and the priests realize that they unknowingly were reversing the drama portrayed in the venerable Hebrew law! Instead of crying to God to look mercifully on their sins, the priests acknowledged their guilt by shouting, "His blood be on us, and on our children." Matthew 27:25.

The law never covers the hypocritical, hence the words, "The ceremony of washing their hands will not cleanse them when by their influence or agency, they have helped to make men drunkards."—Ellen G. White, *Temperance*, p. 28.

To kiss the hand showed love and respect. Judas obviously did not consider that he was fulfilling the prediction, "Kiss the Son, lest he be angry" (Psalm 2:12), in Gethsemane. He, however, prostituted this emblem of affection.

To give one's hand to the other party in an agreement suggested the sharing of interests and purposes. (2 Kings 10:15.) Jeremiah underlines the thought of identifying with another by a handclasp. He recorded in horror that God's people had entered into a solemn compact with Egypt and Assyria by means of this gesture. (Lamentations 5:6.) This giving of the hand still symbolizes the making of a compact, and entering into fellowship. The Holy Spirit is Christ's Agent by whom we become part of the new covenant with God with its attendant freedom and joy.

The hand may speak of will and authority. Kings placed those whom they honored at their right hand. The prophet declared that the Father would exalt His Son to this position (Psalm 110:1), thus sharing His prestige and power with Him. At His ascension Christ sat down at the right hand of God, demonstrating to the universe that He had accomplished His mission for the salvation of man. The indwelling Spirit grants to the Christian victory, prestige, and power. The right hand is an emblem of victory. (Exodus 15:6.) David sang of gracious Omnipotence which granted Israel success under the figure of God's triumphant hand. (Psalms 17:7; 20:6; 44:3.)

The hand may also express displeasure. (Judges 2:15.) The parent spanks his disobedient child with his hand! In Hebrew imagery "the hand of the Lord" is sometimes said to be laid upon men, animals, or even the land in punishment. This expression draws a picture displaying God's frown of censure or judgment. The hand may, therefore, symbolize the discipline meted out to the rebellious by the Holy Spirit. "Therefore is the anger of the Lord kindled against his people, and he hath stretched forth his hand against them, and hath smitten them." Isaiah 5:25.

The hand may also signify the power to carry out involved enterprises. The Lord assured Moses that He would vindicate His people through many marvelous miracles, which He would work before Pharaoh and the Egyptians. These He carried out by His hand. (See Deuteronomy 5:15; 4:34.) He further promised to lead them forth from the control of this despot. Jehovah finally declared that He would drag the recalcitrant pride of Egypt in the dust! All this, Moses realized, would need an authorized and empowered human leader. And so the diffident shepherd of Midian prayed, "Send, I pray thee, by the hand of him whom thou wilt send." Exodus 4:13. But the Lord insisted that he, Moses, must assume this responsibility. Jehovah promised that He would support His representative at all times. When His people expressed doubt, Jehovah asked, "Is the Lord's hand waxed short? thou shalt see now whether my word shall come to pass unto thee or not." Numbers 11:23. This may be put in other words: "Do you think My inspiring Spirit of all these events and their implications is powerless? Now you shall soon see these promises fulfilled." In the same way the Spirit enables the needy soul today to carry out the divine plan for his life. O loving Spirit, come to us! Teach us to trust and believe by the clasp of Thy hand.

The hand may express firmness of purpose. We have an idiom which embraces this idea, "to take a firm hand." This expression suggests that there is no weakness in our resolve. Isaiah noted that God addressed him "with a strong hand." (Isaiah 8:11.) There should be no debate with or disobedience to the divine mandate. We ignore the ministry of the Spirit at grave peril! When God the Holy Ghost gives instructions, we must submit. To resist may lead to the unpardonable sin.

The thought of the transfer of authority is found in the Hebrew gesture of blessing, which the Jews considered most significant. The high priest stretched his hands over all the people when he blessed them. He did this because he could not lay his hand upon each one individually! Then he pronounced the divine benediction. (The actual blessing is found in Numbers 6: 23-27.) Jesus, as God's High Priest, laid His hands upon the little children and blessed them. (Mark 10:16.) He healed by a touch of His hand. Paul's eyesight was restored by the hand of the humble disciple Ananias. (Acts 9:17.) When the apostles, leaders of the new kingdom of priests, invoked the blessing of the Holy Spirit on recently baptized converts, they placed their hands upon them. (Acts 8:17; 19:6.)

The laying on of hands suggested the transfer of identity. This is the meaning of the penitent's role in the ceremony with the lamb, which he brought to the sanctuary as his substitute and sacrifice. The sinner's hands put his guilt upon the innocent victim, which then took his place.

The more honorable consecrates the lesser. For instance, Jehovah, when authorizing Israel's greatest leader for his task, assured Moses that he should be to Aaron "instead of God." (Exodus 4:16.) This fact was demonstrated throughout the service by which Moses consecrated Aaron to the high priesthood. Moses performed all the symbolic acts for his elder brother's elevation to his responsibilities.

One of the deeply significant parts of this rite of priestly consecration was the transfer by Moses to Aaron's hands of the elements of the sacrifice. (Leviticus 8:25-28.) In fact, the most suggestive Hebrew idiom for *consecrate* is "fill the hands." The priest's hands were "filled" with the sacrificed Lamb of God. This stresses identification of interests. Moses also consecrated his political successor, Joshua, by a similar act. (Numbers 27:18.) All that Moses himself stood for as God's representative, he transferred to the next leader of Israel by this gesture. This was also the case with the consecration of the tribe of Levi to the ministry of the sanctuary. (Numbers 8:10.) The Spirit stands ready to grant to Christ's disciples the dynamics of true conversion.

The hand may also indicate fellowship. We shake hands as a token of good will, and thus prove that we carry no concealed weapon! A child may be afraid or lost, but a gentle hand, even of a stranger, placed on his head or shoulder will restore his confidence. A patient in the hospital is terrified of the ordeal of surgery, but the touch of a kindly nurse's hand will calm and reassure him.

General Van Orden once told us at a Columbia Union College chapel of his experience in Puerto Rico as a young lieutenant long years before. His bride of a few months was taken desperately ill. Friends took her to the local Seventh-day Adventist clinic. At home alone, he sat in his living room, greatly agitated. A stranger entered and sat by his side. He put his hand on the young soldier's knee, and they both wept. Calmed and relieved, Van Orden discovered that he was the sympathetic Adventist pastor! By his hand the minister conveyed to the young man the thought that he understood his distress. Mrs. Van Orden got well. The lieutenant decided that wherever he went, he would tell this story to show his appreciation of a Seventh-day Adventist minister's sympathy. The touch of the Spirit's hand gave Daniel and John power and assurance. (Daniel 8:18; 10:10; Revelation 1:17.) By His Spirit, Christ promises to hold our hands and aid us in our every need.

The steady hand calms a frightened animal. It acts in the same way upon a disturbed person. The young prophet Elisha, angered by the willful sin of Jehoshaphat's affinity with Jehoram, the wicked king of Israel, could hardly pray for the beleaguered armies. He felt the need to regain his poise and trust in an overruling Providence. So he called for a minstrel to play quiet music. The prophet reflected for a time on the power of Jehovah. Then the hand of the Lord was laid upon him, and the Spirit gave him the insight and power he needed for the emergency. (2 Kings 3:15.) When Israel and Judah followed his advice, they extricated themselves from their difficulty.

The outstretched hand entreats. David applied this sign to prayer. "I have called daily upon thee," he declared; "I have stretched out my hands unto thee." Psalm 88:9. By His Spirit the Father pleads with His children. He reminds them that He has spread out His hand in loving invitation, to show mercy all the day unto a rebellious people. (Isaiah 65:2.) Under the figure of wisdom, God ever pleads with men to repent. "Turn you at my reproof: behold, I will pour out my spirit unto you, I will make known my words unto you. Because I have called, and ye refused; I have stretched out my hand, and no man regarded; but ye have set at nought all my counsel, and would none of my reproof." Proverbs 1:23-25. The Holy Spirit, Christ's representative on earth, extends God's invitation to us. We reject it if we so choose.

The hand expresses affection. Some of us who are growing older and might need trifocals have forgotten! But we who spend our lives on the various educational campuses are forcefully reminded of this each year. Young people initiate their festival of spring with a touch of their hands! This gesture is generally preceded by the gleam of love-light in their eyes. A squeeze of the hand is perhaps the most common way to whisper, "I love you!" God promises to uphold His people "with the right hand of . . . [His] righteousness." (Isaiah 41:10.) And with the Spirit comes the warmest assurance of divine affection.

God's hand is just as loving and mighty and skillful now as in the ancient days. His promises are certain. "Surely as I have thought," He declares, "so shall it come to pass." "This is the purpose that is purposed upon the whole earth: and this is the hand that is stretched out upon all the nations. For the Lord of hosts hath purposed, and who shall disannul it? and his hand is stretched out, and who shall turn it back?" Isaiah 14:24, 26, 27. His Spirit works mightily today. By His guiding hand He brings all Heaven's purposes to their grand consummation. We should daily ask, Is His hand continually upon me? All that God's hand

Hand—Fellowship of God

plans, the Spirit will accomplish in you. Let us fulfill the conditions outlined by the apostle: "Humble yourselves therefore under the mighty hand of God, that he may exalt you in due time." 1 Peter 5:6. The guarantee is certain: "There is no limit to the usefulness of the one who, putting self aside, makes room for the working of the Holy Spirit upon his heart and lives a life wholly consecrated to God."—*Testimonies*, Vol. 8, p. 19.

God is described as the One who, by His right hand, saves and rescues those afflicted for His name. (Psalms 17:7; 10:12.) In the prophetic picture of the ministry of the Messiah, Jehovah inquires, "Wherefore, when I came was there no man? . . . Is my hand shortened at all, that it cannot redeem?" Isaiah 50:2. Through His Spirit God reaches to the uttermost. He asked the questing Moses, "Is the Lord's hand waxed short? thou shalt see now whether my word shall come to pass unto thee or not." Numbers 11:23. The Spirit who inspires the message will see that it is carried out.

In a very special way God revealed to Moses the illumination of the Spirit. The great leader desired a deeper view of Jehovah's glorious character. The Lord invited him to enter the riven rock —a symbol of the "Rock of Ages cleft for me." Across its entrance He placed His hand. Through it Moses was shown all that he was able to discern of God's glory. What a thrilling parable of salvation! Through the nail-pierced hand of God's Son, the Spirit today will enable us to behold the fullness of His glory too. May God give us discernment!

Eternal Spirit, gentle hand of our blessed Saviour in the world today, how we appreciate Thy blessed ministry!

14.

BREATH --
Life of God

Breath is the inspiration and exhalation of air by the lungs. By this process the blood takes up life-giving oxygen and by it vivifies every fiber of our bodies. In turn, many of the waste products of the body are transferred to the breath and exhaled. This process is essential for the life of man and continues until death.

The atmosphere we breathe is absolutely vital to life. We can live without food for weeks. We can survive for days without water. But cut off our supply of air, and we die in a matter of minutes! This air is a well-balanced mixture of essential gases and is made according to the divine recipe. Change this formula, even a little, and discomfort and death result. All around us smog, pollen, dust, and industrial gases make breathing difficult. Pure air is exhilarating.

Let us consider the effects of breathing in various phases of the life cycle. Our moment-by-moment living produces wastes in the cells. The bloodstream catches up these discarded substances and carries them to our lungs. Breathing helps to rid the body of this burned-up fuel. In this marvelous exchange machine, these useless and poisonous materials turn into carbon dioxide gas and

BREATH—LIFE OF GOD

are exhaled. This outbreathing is nature's method for purifying the stream of life and helps to keep the tissue clean.

Deep breathing brings clean air into our systems. Through the purified bloodstream it ventilates every part of our beings. Our bodies, therefore, constantly need full drafts of pure air. Breathing also helps in combating disease. For these reasons we should try to establish the habit of inhaling deeply. Unless we do this, superficial breathing will soon become a way of life. All these rules for effective physical breathing have overtones in our spiritual lives.

Breathing consists of two activities. The first is external. We drink in the air about us. This activity may be noisy, as when we hurry and gasp for breath. Or it may be quiet. Then there is internal breathing, the process by which the blood cells breathe when absorbing the oxygen we have taken into our lungs. In this process the cells give off carbon dioxide into the blood. This carries it to the lungs, where in turn it is exhaled. This silent and involuntary process continues as long as life lasts.

In the spiritual as in the physical life, vigorous exertion produces a need for much more air. Sometimes in emergencies, as when diving or swimming underwater, we gasp for oxygen in order to survive. Spiritually there are many who are gasping for the breath of life. God longs to breathe into them His Spirit, but unlike our involuntary daily breathing, we must actually want to partake of the life of the Spirit. We must choose to breathe before His life-bringing presence can fill us.

Breathing consists of inspiration as well as expiration. We must take in the oxygen before we can breathe out the carbon dioxide. The life-sustaining element must enter before the toxins are cleared away. This is true of our Christian life. We must partake of the Spirit's power before the current of our thoughts and the tendency of our acts can be purified. We must breathe in the atmosphere of heaven before the lurking, poisonous miasma of temptation and sin is dispelled.

Breathing continues ceaselessly throughout life. Should oxygen fail to reach the brain, it ceases to function in a few minutes. Even if physical life survives, the person becomes a mere vegetable, incapable of carrying out his normal functions. So without the Spirit constantly in our lives, we become merely a spiritual vegetable unable even to choose to fulfill God's will for us.

Breath is essential to life and symbolizes Jehovah's power. Let us consider carefully some thoughts which grow out of this idea. In his argument with Job, Elihu noted, "The spirit of God hath made me, and the breath of the Almighty hath given me life." Job 33:4. The psalmist endorses this concept in his song of God's work in nature, "Thou sendest forth thy spirit, they are created." Psalm 104:30. David observed that all the varied forms of animate creatures exist because of "the breath of his mouth." (Psalm 33:6.) The Scriptures are unanimous that breath symbolizes the Spirit's life-giving and life-sustaining power. Ellen G. White recommended the attitude which all Christians should cultivate when she said that they "need to know from experience what the Holy Spirit will do for them. It will bless the receiver, and make him a blessing. It is sad that every soul is not praying for the vital breath of the Spirit, for we are ready to die if it breathe not on us."—*Testimonies to Ministers*, p. 64.

Man depends on God for every breath he takes. In his near-fatal sickness, Job resolved that "all the while my breath is in me, and the spirit of God is in my nostrils; my lips shall not speak wickedness." (Job 27:3, 4.) Here the patriarch equated breath and the Spirit. This thought recalls the story of the origin of the human family. Inspiration records that "the Lord God formed man of the dust of the ground, and breathed into his nostrils the breath of life; and man became a living soul." (Genesis 2:7.) And while this entire process of creation was taking place, the Spirit "brooded." (Genesis 1:2, margin.)

The breath of life, as we have noted, is also termed the "breath of the Almighty." El Shaddai, the Hebrew name also

Breath—Life of God

translated Almighty God, is a title of Deity filled with richest allusions. Its root is the word for a mother's breasts, warm with comfort and rich with sustenance for her helpless babe. El Shaddai, Job recalled, shared with insensate clay the mystery of His life by a personal act of creation. Through the Holy Spirit's power, man is to live the life lent to him by God. Both his physical and spiritual well-being are dependent upon the breath of God.

At Olivet, Jesus bade His disciples farewell. In His final benediction He said, "Peace be unto you: as my Father hath sent me, even so send I you. And when he had said this, he breathed on them, and saith unto them, Receive ye the Holy Ghost." John 20:21, 22. This is the first allusion to breath of God in the New Testament. At Pentecost the Christian church began to live for God. As their dynamic, the apostles received the Spirit of Christ, or the Spirit of Jesus. The word *receive,* as used by our Lord, may with equal accuracy be translated "take ye." The disciples had their part to act. They might choose to accept or discard the proffered power, for God never forces His gifts upon His people. The ability to witness, to "bind" and "loose," Christ bestows upon His followers. All the activities of the spiritual life depend on the breath of God.

When a man ceases to breathe, decay and death immediately take over his body. Physicians must start his breathing again within a very few minutes, or brain damage will become irreparable. Even if we continue breathing, but breathe foul air, our brains and bodies will become feeble and incapable of vigorous and creative activity. People in an unventilated room grow sleepy. This is true of the Christian life also. Today, "people need the breath of life breathed into them, that they may arouse to spiritual action," Ellen G. White declared. She continued, "Many have lost their vital energy; they are sluggish, dead, as it were. Let those who have been receiving the grace of Christ help these souls to arouse to action. Let us keep in the current of life that comes from Christ, that we may kindle life in some other soul."—*Review and Herald,* April 28, 1904.

Breath is essential for speech. Christian witnessing depends on the breath of God. The Spirit in the heart puts Heaven's message on the lips. This chain reaction has always been so. In ancient times holy men spoke when they were inspired, or breathed through, and moved, or borne along, by the Spirit. (See 2 Peter 1:21; 2 Timothy 3:16.) The spreading of the message of Heaven today requires the same dynamic as it did in its initial proclamation. "There is a great work to do; and the Spirit of the living God must enter into the living messenger, that the truth may go with power. Without the Holy Spirit, without the breath of God, there is torpidity of conscience, loss of spiritual life."—Ellen G. White, in *Review and Herald,* December 3, 1908. That the church today may fulfill her commission to proclaim Christ's evangel to a darkened world, she needs the breath of God. Without His abiding power, no effective witness is possible.

This breathing of the Holy Spirit into men by Christ constituted a sharing of His very life with them. "Before the disciples could fulfill their official duties in connection with the church, Christ breathed His Spirit upon them. He was committing to them a most sacred trust, and He desired to impress them with the fact that without the Holy Spirit this work could not be accomplished.

"The Holy Spirit is the breath of spiritual life in the soul. The impartation of the Spirit is the impartation of the life of Christ. It imbues the receiver with the attributes of Christ. Only those who are thus taught of God, those who possess the inward working of the Spirit, and in whose life the Christ-life is manifested, are to stand as representative men, to minister in behalf of the church."—*The Desire of Ages,* p. 805. The empowering breath of God which our Lord shares with His people is His own life. He thus places within us His very principles. As the life-giving oxygen purifies and energizes every cell in the body, so the breath of God brings the power of Christ into our inmost thoughts and feelings and purifies them to perform His service. Then "in him we live, and move, and have our being." (Acts 17:28.)

Until the baby begins to breathe, it is unable to take its place in independent human existence. How breath takes over and the babe begins to live provides one of the glorious mysteries of life. The coming of the spiritual breath into the disciple's heart to enable the newborn babe in Christ to live for his Master is a mystery. "When the Holy Spirit works the human agent, it does not ask us in what way it shall operate. Often it moves in unexpected ways. . . . The Jews refused to receive Christ, because He did not come in accordance with their expectations."—*Testimonies to Ministers,* p. 64. The development of the life of the Spirit in the Christian is as mysterious as the growth of physical life in an embryo. The unborn babe progresses silently in darkness, stage by stage, and eventually passes from its initial environment into fuller and richer spheres of existence. So must the aspiring Christian.

But this illustration is incomplete. The Christian must exercise his power of choice moment by moment. We have the option of breathing the pure, life-giving atmosphere of Heaven or the miasma of unbelief, doubt, and evil surmising. "We must rise above the frosty atmosphere in which we have hitherto lived, and with which Satan would surround our souls," Ellen White stressed, "and breathe in the hallowed atmosphere of heaven." —*Review and Herald,* May 6, 1890. Thus our spiritual natures will mature. The moment-by-moment ministry of the Spirit is vital for this.

Once he has started in the Christian way, the disciple's responsibilities do not end. Day by day the Christian must continually choose which atmosphere he will inhale. Satan ever breathes his hellish breath into all whom he can influence, but Christ stands ready to infuse the very air of heaven into anyone who will surrender and accept Him. The decision as to which spirit we shall receive is always open to each one of us, and we must exercise this choice.

The sower sows seed. Christ often likened the growth of Christian experience to the steady development of a seed. "For a time the good seed may lie unnoticed in the heart, giving no evidence that it has taken root; but afterward, as the Spirit of God breathes on the soul, the hidden seed springs up, and at last brings forth fruit."—*Education,* p. 105. The Holy Spirit is Heaven's generative force in the soul. Without His constant ministry we shall never bring forth fruit.

To achieve this, man must cooperate with God. The daily growth in grace requires personal and constant effort on the part of the Christian. He must keep his heart in tune with Heaven. Moment by moment his mind must be ready to speed prayers for the Spirit's help to the throne of grace. Thus he gains the victory in daily experience and is sanctified.

We are given this inspired preview of the Christians who are earnestly preparing for their Lord's coming. "Those who rose up with Jesus would send up their faith to Him in the holiest, and pray, 'My Father, give us Thy Spirit.' Then Jesus would breathe upon them the Holy Ghost. In that breath was light, power, and much love, joy, and peace." Ellen White then wrote concerning another group, "I turned to look at the company who were still bowed before the throne; they did not know that Jesus had left it. Satan appeared to be by the throne, trying to carry on the work of God. I saw them look up to the throne, and pray, 'Father, give us Thy Spirit.' Satan would then breathe upon them an unholy influence; in it there was light and much power, but no sweet love, joy, and peace. Satan's object was to keep them deceived and to draw back and deceive God's children."—*Early Writings,* pp. 55, 56. The Spirit is Heaven's sweet influence in the soul. His presence and power alone fit human life for translation.

Breath—Life of God

Breathing may be a silent process. The breath of God may also be voiceless! Jesus said to Nicodemus that "the Spirit breatheth where it will." (John 3:8, margin, A.R.V.) He then added, "Thou canst not tell——" The Spirit inbreathes His life in quietness and peace. Vivified by this breath, man continually grows imperceptibly. Only by the fruit can we measure progress.

The Spirit of God is essential for success in Christian witnessing. This was vividly illustrated in a vision granted to Ezekiel. (Ezekiel 37:1-14.) The prophet was led by God's angel to a somber valley. To his horror he noted that it was filled with dry bones! Vast quantities of them were on every hand. When asked whether he thought it possible for the bones to live again, Ezekiel exclaimed in effect, "Only God knows!"

Then the Lord bade His servant preach to them the words of life. What an audience—dry bones! In response to his message there were noise and movement. This activity led to cooperation. Each bone found and fitted itself to its mate! Soon a skeletal army stood before the prophet, and, as Ezekiel continued to preach, flesh formed to cover these bare bones. Each soldier was soon complete in every visible essential. But he lacked life!

At this point God ordered His messenger to pray for the Spirit. "Come from the four winds, O breath, and breathe upon these slain, that they may live." In answer to his petition the breath of God flooded the silent vale of death and gave life to those who had been cut down in the battle with sin.

This acted parable has a rich message for us. Ellen White observed, "The Spirit of God, with its vivifying power, must be in every human agent, that every spiritual muscle and sinew may be in exercise. Without the Holy Spirit, without the breath of God, there is torpidity of conscience, loss of the spiritual life. . . . Unless there is genuine conversion of the soul to God; unless the vital breath of God quickens the soul to spiritual life; unless the professors of truth are actuated by heaven-born principle, they are not born of the incorruptible seed which liveth and abideth forever. Unless they trust in the righteousness of Christ as their only security; unless they copy His character, labor in His spirit, they are naked, they have not on the robe of His righteousness. The dead are often made to pass for the living; for those who are working out what they term salvation after their own ideas, have not God working in them to will and to do of His good pleasure. This class is well represented by the valley of dry bones Ezekiel saw in vision. Those who have had committed to them the treasures of truth, and yet who are dead in trespasses and sin, need to be created anew in Christ Jesus."—*Review and Herald,* January 17, 1893.

The message of God to those represented as dead in their sins is one of hope. They may live again! The new birth, or conversion, the Lord desires for each of His children. This is the only way to the ultimate fulfillment of God's purpose. The Lord promises, through Ezekiel, "[I] shall put my spirit in you, and ye shall live, and I shall place you in your own land." Ezekiel 37:14. Many other illustrations in the Scriptures strengthen this assurance. Let us consider a few of them.

Spiritual artificial respiration is important in certain conditions. The pride and joy of a mother's heart lay lifeless in her arms. Elisha's empty room, in which so many prayers had ascended, mocked her with its impotence. She laid the still form of her son on the prophet's bed and hurried out to find him. When she met him, her word was so very brief that he only partly comprehended her. Elisha then dispatched Gehazi to her house with the prophet's rod, emblem of authority and power. The servant hurried into the room of death and laid the rod on the boy, but nothing happened.

When the prophet, brooding in sorrow, reached the home, his heart went out with sympathy to the family. Going to the quiet form in his familiar room, Elisha lay upon the lad, his eyes on the boy's, his hands on his. Heart to heart, body to body, the living and the dead met. The identification was symbolically com-

Breath—Life of God

plete. The prophet's mature fingers rested on the lad's. His adult eyes looked where the boy's gaze should be fixed. His mouth breathed living breath into the unresponsive body, and the boy lived! (2 Kings 4:18-37.) Where the rod had failed, identification and love and sympathy succeeded. The breath of the Almighty, through His chosen instrument, brought life back to the lad.

Another thrilling account of the power of spiritual artificial respiration concerns Eutychus, a typical young man. Even when the famous and eloquent Apostle Paul preached, he sat on the windowsill as far away from him as possible! Eutychus could not be more out of the room and still be inside. And then he went to sleep. How many descendants he has today! His behavior is the sure way to suicide. Eutychus died in a religious service because he did not try to pay attention to what was going on. Now mark what the preacher did not do. He did not reprimand his parents for not keeping him awake. He did not scold his schoolteachers for not inculcating more respect into him. He did not criticize his companions for not setting him a better example or the members of the church for not being more interested in him. Paul left his pulpit and went down to the level on which Eutychus was lying. While others wept and lamented that a wonderful life of promise had been prematurely cut off, the apostle "identified" himself with the lad. Like Elisha, he lay on him, looked through his eyes, felt as he felt, breathed as he breathed, and, if you please, shared his life with the boy. And *he* lived! (Acts 20:7-12.) This is the way the Spirit always works. He comes and shares His life with those dead in sin and gives them the life which comes from above.

The Spirit works through His chosen and cooperative helpers. Our Saviour long ago gave us the divine method. He promised to send the Spirit to His disciples, and added, "And when he is come [to you, the context suggests], he will convince [margin] the world of sin, and of righteousness, and of judgment." John 16:8. The Spirit uses human instruments. Isn't it thrilling to think that we might be at the right place and at the right time to give spiritual artificial respiration to some soul in need?

"The Holy Spirit ever abides with him who is seeking for perfection of Christian character. The Holy Spirit furnishes the pure motive, the living, active principle, that sustains striving, wrestling, believing souls in every emergency and under every temptation. The Holy Spirit sustains the believer amid the world's hatred, amid the unfriendliness of relatives, amid disappointment, amid the realization of imperfection, and amid the mistakes of life. Depending upon the matchless purity and perfection of Christ, the victory is sure to him who looks unto the Author and Finisher of our faith."—Ellen G. White, in *Review and Herald*, November 30, 1897.

We may help others gain this victory by keeping our minds alert to souls in need. Then we should testify of the life and experience the Spirit has given us. He will use us to infuse His presence and power into those in sin.

When all this has been said, another point must be stressed. "It is not the human agent that is to inspire with life. The Lord God of Israel will do that part, quickening the lifeless spiritual nature into activity. The breath of the Lord of hosts must enter into the lifeless bodies. In the judgment, when all secrets are laid bare, it will be known that the voice of God spoke through the human agent, and aroused the torpid conscience, and stirred the lifeless faculties, and moved sinners to repentance and contrition, and forsaking of sins. It will then be clearly seen that through the human agent, faith in Jesus Christ was imparted to the soul, and spiritual life from heaven was breathed upon one who was dead in trespasses and sins, and he was quickened with spiritual life."—*Ibid.*, January 17, 1893.

Nature abhors a vacuum. Where one exists, air is ready to rush in. Empty lungs, too, long to be filled with clean, fresh air. Christ illustrated this truth with an intriguing parable. "When the unclean spirit is gone out of a man," He said, "he walketh through dry places, seeking rest, and findeth none. Then he saith, I will return into my house from whence I came out; and when he is come, he findeth it empty, swept, and garnished. Then goeth he, and taketh with himself seven other spirits more wicked than himself, and they enter in and dwell there: and the last state of that man is worse than the first." Matthew 12:43-45.

Ellen White interestingly observed on this thought: "It is not enough to make the heart empty: we must have the vacuum filled with the love of God. The soul must be furnished with the graces of the Spirit of God. We may leave off many bad habits, and yet not be truly sanctified, because we do not have a connection with God. We must unite with Christ. There is a reservoir of power at our command, and we are not to remain in the dark, cold, sunless cave of unbelief; or we shall not catch the bright beams of the Sun of Righteousness."—*Ibid.*, January 24, 1893. If the newly cleansed lungs of spiritual life do not breathe the air of Heaven, they will soon gasp for the alien winds of spurious doctrines and destructive philosophies.

Should the gospel worker ever allow outward appearances to deter his efforts? Inspiration has this reply: "The souls of those whom we desire to save are like the representation which Ezekiel saw in vision—a valley of dry bones. They are dead in trespasses and sins, but God would have us deal with them as though they were living. Were the question put to us, 'Son of man, can these bones live?' our answer would be only the confession of ignorance. 'O Lord, Thou knowest.' To all appearance there is nothing to lead us to hope for their restoration. Yet nevertheless the word of the prophecy must be spoken even to those who are like the dry bones in the valley. We are in no wise to be deterred from fulfilling our commission by the listlessness, the dullness, the lack of spiritual perception, in those upon whom the Word of God is brought to bear. We are to preach the word of life to those whom we may judge to be as hopeless subjects as though they were in their graves. Though they may seem unwilling to hear or to receive the light of truth, without questioning or wavering we are to do our part. . . .

"But not only does this simile of the dry bones apply to the world, but also to those who have been blessed with great light; for they also are like the skeletons of the valley. They have the form of men, the framework of the body; but they have not spiritual life. But the parable does not leave the dry bones merely knit together into the forms of men; for it is not enough that there is symmetry of limb and feature. The breath of life must vivify the bodies, that they may stand upright, and spring into activity. These bones represent the house of Israel, the church of God, and the hope of the church is the vivifying influence of the Holy Spirit. The Lord must breathe upon the dry bones, that they may live."—*Ibid.*, January 17, 1893.

"Breathe on me, Breath of God,
  Fill me with life anew,
That I may love what Thou dost love,
  And do what Thou wouldst do.

"Breathe on me, Breath of God,
  Until my heart is pure,
Until with Thee I will one will,
  To do and to endure.

"Breathe on me, Breath of God,
  Till I am wholly Thine,
Until this earthly part of me
  Glows with Thy fire divine.

"Breathe on me, Breath of God,
  So shall I constant be,
And live with Thee the perfect life
  Of Thine eternity."

—*Edwin Hatch.*

15.

FINGER --
Guidance of God

We use our fingers to perform amazing tasks. We can train them to carry out the most accurate measurements, to detect the difference between one and two sheets of the thinnest paper. The fingers of a musician produce beautiful tonal effects. The fingers of the blind can be taught to read! The fingers of the artist can almost duplicate the rainbow! Precision and dexterity characterize the quality of the work of our fingers. The finger is our most personal and carefully controlled tool.

God permits Himself to be described anthropomorphically. "The eyes of the Lord are in every place, beholding the evil and the good." Proverbs 15:3. His ears are ever open to hear man's cry. (Psalm 34:15.) His arms strengthen (Psalm 89:21), and His hand delivers (Deuteronomy 5:15). Even God's finger, we shall notice, illustrates the special workings of His providence. As the hand of God suggests power employed generally, His finger symbolizes activity used in its concentrated and precisely directed energy.

If you compare Luke's account of our Lord's casting out of a devil which caused dumbness with that given by Matthew (Luke 11:20; Matthew 12:28), you will see that Jesus used the expression "finger of God" as an emblem of a special function of the Holy Spirit.

The occasion in which Christ employed these words occurred during an argument between the Pharisees and the Saviour. The rulers of Israel strove to undermine Christ's authority as the Messiah. They had spread the rumor that He cast out devils by the authority of Beelzebub! By using the expression "finger of God" Jesus designed to turn the minds of the more thoughtful of His hearers back to the episodes connected with the deliverance of Israel from the bondage of Egypt, and their original establishment as a nation. God had empowered Moses to turn his rod into a serpent. This was evidence of his divine authority to organize and lead God's people. The Egyptian magicians, however, made it appear that they could do the same wonders with their rods. But when Moses later performed feats of which they were incapable, the sorcerers exclaimed, "This is the finger of God!" Exodus 8:19.

In these words they described the working of a Power whose operations went beyond both their understanding and their ability to reproduce. Jesus used this ancient phrase to call attention to the fact that even heathen sorcerers long ago had acknowledged a power they could not explain. He implied that the Pharisees of His day were actually rejecting obvious evidences of the workings of God when they demanded further signs of His Messiahship. These rulers should have inferred that the Saviour was condemning their lack of insight, and implying that their infidelity actually surpassed that of the Egyptian magicians at the time of the Exodus! Evidences of divine authority invested in Moses, He said in effect, had then been disbelieved in pagan Egypt. Greater evidences of the visible Messiah Israelites in Jerusalem were now ignoring. In all periods of Biblical history the finger of God has been the symbol of the Agent who presents evidence to validate Heaven's representatives. To reject these credentials meant denying the Spirit. Let us open wide our eyes

Finger—Guidance of God

to discern the workings of God's finger in the world today.

Moses, shut in by Jehovah's glory in the heights of Sinai, received from the hands of his Maker the two tables of the law. Meanwhile, Israel in the valley, wrapped up in mammon, worshiped the golden calf. Upon the flaming mountain God's finger traced divine requirements on stone tablets. In the desert valley man's rebellious mind and body adored a calf of gold. What a parable of life these contrasts present! How are we treating what His Spirit writes today?

Today the Holy Spirit longs to impress these ten precepts on man's surrendered heart. Then, having given His laws, the Lord stands ready to help His people carry them out. The wise man gave his son this advice: "Keep my commandments, and live. . . . Bind them upon thy fingers, write them upon the table of thine heart." Proverbs 7:2, 3.

But unlike the finger-written stone tablets of the law, we must cooperate with the Spirit if we would be impressed with the principles of the kingdom and attain the true goals of life. Up in the mount God's finger delineated what constituted righteousness. Yet in the valley men adored an image which their own fingers had fashioned! How careful we should be to allow the Spirit-indicted laws of God to regulate the work of our fingers. The divine finger stands ready today to trace the details of God's will on the tablets of our minds.

Awe-inspiring signs that a supernatural Being was on the mountain accompanied the giving of the law. At the summit of Sinai lightning flashed and trumpets shrilled. In strange indifference, in the valley of sin, the timbrel clashed, and faces flushed in passion. Israel turned their backs on these evidences of the divine Presence at the very moment when God was actually tracing, with His finger, the letters which would spell the sinner's doom. The finger of God was His agency for pointing out the standards of His kingdom. These man must bind to his heart so that his motives may be pure.

The finger of God inspired His servants with the Spirit of prophecy to do their wonderful work. Ellen White noted: "In my books, the truth is stated, barricaded by a 'Thus saith the Lord.' The Holy Spirit traced these truths upon my heart and mind as indelibly as the law was traced by the finger of God, upon the tables of stone, which are now in the ark, to be brought forth in that great day when sentence will be pronounced against every evil, seducing science produced by the father of lies."—*Colporteur Ministry*, p. 126. The Spirit's finger points to God's truth for our study and acceptance.

On one occasion Jesus was teaching in a portico of the Temple when a group of scribes and Pharisees attracted His attention. Dragging a woman into His presence, they accused her of the grossest sin. They harshly demanded Christ's immediate verdict. They hoped to stab Him on one of the horns of a dilemma. According to Hebrew law, the adulteress and her lover should both be stoned, but these Jewish leaders accused only the woman. By Roman rule she was free. Should Christ condemn her to death, He would incur Roman censure. Should He spare her, they hoped to rouse nationalistic feelings against Him for repudiating their law. Jesus stooped down and with His finger wrote in the dust. Intrigued, the Scribes and Pharisees crowded about the Saviour to see what He was doing. Each was shocked to read his secret sins in the catalog Christ had made. One by one, each slunk away in shame. This time the finger of God traced, in transient dust, the sins of man. Christ might have inscribed these crimes in imperishable granite. He might have engraved them with the point of a diamond in immemorial rock. But He recorded them in the lightest dust, evidence so easily erased by the first breath of wind or washed away by the first shower of rain! So compassionate is Christ! In this instance the finger of God was the agency for noting man's failures.

Belshazzar's feast was at its riotous height (Daniel 5:1, 2) when the king blasphemously attempted to show how much he despised Daniel's God. His grandfather, Nebuchadnezzar, had accorded all honor for Babylon's greatness to Jehovah. (Daniel 4:34-37.) But Belshazzar refused to acknowledge the true God. Suddenly, bloodless fingers traced upon the plastered wall of the banquet hall the sentence of Babylon's doom. Four cryptic words appeared. To interpret these words, Daniel was summoned. "Weighed and wanting," was his verdict.

God's finger today warns of judgments to come on "Babylon the great." The task of the Spirit is threefold. He convinces the world of sin by pointing out error. He teaches righteousness by indicating the divine standard of conduct. He warns of judgment to come by assuring us that a day of reckoning is inevitable. (John 16:8.)

To the psalmist creation spoke of creation's God. "When I consider thy heavens," he exclaimed, "the work of thy fingers, the moon and the stars, which thou hast ordained; what is man, that thou art mindful of him?" Psalm 8:3, 4. The finger of God formed the universe with precision. The Spirit created man with finish. To set all these works in operation "the Spirit of God moved upon the face of the waters." (Genesis 1:2.) The finger of God was the divine Agency for making growing objects instinct with life and light.

Also in Israel's ritual the finger applied the consecrating unguent to the ear and thumb and toe of cleansed lepers (Leviticus 14:14), and then it sprinkled more oil before God's presence (verse 27). Today, through His Spirit, Jesus enables the cleansed sinner's ear to heed God's voice, his hand to work His will, and his foot to walk His way. The finger is Christ's agent for making effective the full results and benefits of His atonement.

The censorious use their fingers to point out those whom they think are wrongdoers, and often they condemn the innocent. Isaiah couples the yoke of bondage and the finger of accusation. (Isaiah 58:9.) God's Spirit, however, never condemns falsely. While He knows all hearts, He yet intercedes with groanings which cannot be put into human language, but which eloquently plead for mercy before God. (Romans 8:26.)

In the parable of the rich man and Lazarus, Christ described an unfortunate in torment as longing in vain for a kindly fingertip, moistened with cooling water, to relieve his parched tongue. (Luke 16:24.) Our Lord pointed out the folly of this vain hope. He who does not slake his thirst at God's spring in this life, will search in vain for solace in the next. (Verse 31.) The finger of God today will grant us rivers of living water so that we need never thirst again. Should we reject the Spirit's appeals in this life, we shall find no cooling finger in the next.

God's finger points. It teaches by emphasizing. So the Spirit guides us into all truth. When the Christian questions which way to turn, God's eloquent finger gives him directions. (Isaiah 30:21; Psalm 25:9.) The only safe path is the way He wishes us to go.

The finger may gesture reproof. The finger of God warns of sin and danger. (John 16:7-11.) When tempted to speak without due thought, to act without due consideration, to run without due direction, to do without due knowledge, to condemn without due evidence, look up, and the finger will be upraised to warn. The Still, Small Voice will steady with the whispered word, Beware! The finger of God shapes character and records conduct. He indicates and warns. He endows and opens. Heed His messages.

The sculptor uses his fingers to mold the clay. With a deft touch here and gentle pressure there, he adds details to the face he is delineating, and strength and character shine out of the expression he depicts in his statue. The Lord is the Great Sculptor. With His finger He forms our characters and gives expression to our lives. He is reproducing the likeness of Christ in us day by day. Our part is to yield to Him and to become what His finger fashions.

The potter uses his fingers to fashion his various vessels on his wheel. Sometimes a small stone in the clay will mar the pot he is forming. Then his dexterous fingers will fashion another vessel. Jehovah takes this illustration and applies it to the ministry of the Holy Ghost. The divine finger, skilled and ready, shapes the rough clay of our lives into the perfect vessel God designs us to become. He wishes to fill us with His grace and then to bear the provisions of redeeming love to those in need. But, and this point must be stressed, we must continually yield to the shaping, disciplining touch of the Spirit. Our danger is that we shall resist or reject His workings.

We greatly need the Holy Spirit's guiding presence. We should invite Him to write the divine precepts with the stylus of God's Word upon the yielded clay tablets of our wills. He is Heaven's Scribe. Allow His finger to trace His message upon your inmost life. Only thus do we become living epistles, freighted with the story of salvation, seen and read by all men.

We should ever be on the alert to discover where His finger points as our divine Guide. Christ's healing finger will touch our ears to heed His message—He is the divine Physician. His empowering finger will impress our tongues with His heavenly words—He is the divine Prompter. And in the hereafter, we shall be unafraid, for His pen will record our actions in the book of life, and we shall remain hidden in Christ, dwelt in by Christ, and triumphant in Christ. We should constantly pray, "O Spirit, fill our lives now."

FINGER OF GOD

Finger Divine, touch Thou my *eyes,*
    and I shall see Thy child, not tree, mere thing,
    but blood-bought prince of God, and seeing, rejoice, when,
Finger Divine, Thou touch my eyes.

Finger Divine, touch Thou my *ears,*
    and I shall hear Thy voice, not siren's call,

but trump angelical, and hearing, obey, when,
Finger Divine, Thou touch my ears.

Finger Divine, touch Thou my *lips*,
    and I shall sing Thy praise, not sin's soft song,
    but hymn of power great, and singing, adore, when,
Finger Divine, Thou touch my lips.

Finger Divine, touch Thou my *hands*,
    and I shall do Thy work, not sin-filled deed,
    but daily task of love, and doing, repeat, when,
Finger Divine, Thou touch my hands.

Finger Divine, touch Thou my *feet*,
    and I shall walk Thy way, not deathward road,
    but rugged path to light, and walking, march on, when,
Finger Divine, Thou touch my feet.

Finger Divine, touch Thou my *heart*,
    and I shall know Thy peace, not longing vain,
    but heaven's calm serene, and knowing, repose, when,
Finger Divine, Thou touch my heart.

                                                        Amen.

16.

EYE --
Discernment of God

The eye is one of the most indispensable organs of the body, and its loss one of the greatest misfortunes we can suffer. We use our eyes to perform every task. We observe objects, judge colors and distances, discriminate between items, all with our eyes. We need them for protection as we move through life. They help us avoid dangers and pitfalls. They enable us to maintain our equilibrium and aid in every step we take. In order to touch and taste, we must come into actual contact with objects. The eye, on the other hand, may receive its sensation from things at very great distances. We can even see heavenly bodies millions of light years away! The eye is a most versatile organ. Our ears can hear only within a limited spectrum of vibrations. But "the eye can see objects which may be a million times different in brightness," for instance, the sun and a piece of coal.

Scriptural imagery uses the eye as a symbol of the Holy Spirit. In his vision of the throne of the universe, John caught a glimpse of the Lamb of God having "seven eyes." These, he explained, "are the seven Spirits of God" (Revelation 5:6), a descriptive phrase for the Holy Ghost. (Revelation 1:4. Verses 4 and 5 list the three Persons of the Trinity.)

The Bible uses seven as a figure expressing perfection. "The number seven indicates completeness, and is symbolic."—*The Acts of the Apostles*, p. 585. The sevenfold Spirit depicts the perfection and completeness of His ministry. Through the empowering of the Holy Ghost, Christ, the resurrected Man, has perfect sight—hindsight, insight, and foresight.

Zechariah stresses the same thought. He, too, viewed the judgment scene. In it the Stone or Rock, Christ Jesus, had "seven eyes." (Zechariah 3:9.) The prophet explained this illustration in the words, "They are the eyes of the Lord, which run to and fro through the whole earth." (Zechariah 4:10.) The eye symbolizes that aspect of the Spirit's ministry which sees what God deems should be perceived everywhere. The Spirit possesses omniscience. "The eyes of the Lord are in every place, beholding the evil and the good." Proverbs 15:3. Nothing is hidden from His all-searching eye. At the judgment all will realize that God's all-seeing eye reads their hearts.

Perhaps the most impressive aspect of the function of God's eye is His ability to see the end from the beginning. The Spirit possesses prescience. Through His ministry he empowered prophets to view events long in the future. By means of His inspired writers, the Lord provided hope and guidance to all. Ellen White noted that "the eye of God, looking down the ages, was fixed upon the crisis which His people are to meet, when earthly powers shall be arrayed against them."—*The Great Controversy*, p. 634. The Spirit has given mankind a world view of coming events.

The foresight granted by the inspiring Spirit enabled Paul to see that "bonds and afflictions" awaited him at Jerusalem. (Acts 20:23.) This awareness of lurking dangers, accompanied by previews of God's overall designs, strengthens man's confidence in divine leadership. (1 Samuel 10:2-10.) These illustrations show that this foresight of the Spirit may be, on occasion, bestowed on individuals. As we journey through life, we should pray for

Eye—Discernment of God

the presence of the Spirit so that we may see the waymarks clearly.

Step by step our eyes scrutinize the path we tread. This thought led Job to affirm, "I was eyes to the blind." Job 29:15. He gave directions and assistance to those who did not know which way to turn. As Israel journeyed through the desert, uncertainties and problems beset their path. High above them the pillar of cloud by day and fire by night led the way, but the indications of the road to travel were too general. On the ground steep hills and deep and rough valleys appeared before the people. Occasionally questions arose concerning which might be the better path to follow as the beacon led onward.

Jethro (also called Hobab), the father-in-law of Moses, paid a visit to his daughter and grandchildren. Moses immediately realized the immense value his knowledge of the terrain and experience in coping with the problems of the desert would be to Israel. He reminded Jethro that the hosts of God were traveling to the place designated by Jehovah Himself centuries before. He extended Jethro an invitation. "Come thou with us, and we will do thee good." "Leave us not, I pray thee; forasmuch as thou knowest how we are to encamp in the wilderness, and thou mayest be to us instead of eyes." Numbers 10:29, 31. What an honor! Moses invited Jethro to be the "eyes" of Israel. His understanding and wisdom are implicit in this figure.

God has promised His disciples the Spirit's eyes to "guide . . . [them] into all truth." (John 16:13.) The Holy Ghost is mankind's heavenly Pilot. He understands every hidden difficulty in the voyage of life. Christ has granted us the whole framework of inspired knowledge in the Holy Scriptures. From the Bible the Spirit brings to the individual Christian an understanding of the precise path he should tread. Day by day He guides the trusting feet of the true disciple steadily toward the Promised Land. The Lord is ever ready to fulfill His promise, "I will instruct thee and teach thee in the way which thou shalt go: I will guide thee with mine eye." Psalm 32:8. The guidance of the Holy Spirit is infallible. Let us follow Him closely. Christ, as the Pillar of fire by night and the Cloud of shade by day, leads the Christian church through the wilderness of sin. The Spirit, the eye of God, aids, advises, and comforts each pilgrim, enabling him to follow his Lord along a safe path.

The Spirit of God scrutinizes everything. He is Heaven's Overseer. Job testified that "his eyes are upon the ways of man, and he seeth all his goings. There is no darkness, nor shadow of death, where the workers of iniquity may hide themselves." (Job 34:21, 22.) Solomon further attests this omniscience, "The ways of man are before the eyes of the Lord, and he pondereth all his goings." Proverbs 5:21. He adds, "The eyes of the Lord are in every place, beholding the evil and the good." Proverbs 15:3. The Spirit discerns everything in heaven and on earth. This clear vision He willingly shares with all who will receive Him. His power enables their eyes also to discern the good and the bad. How careful we should always be to do "that which is right in the eyes of the Lord." (Deuteronomy 13:18.)

It is possible to blind ourselves. He who refuses to look will lose the power to see. This is witnessed by the pit ponies employed in some Welsh coal mines. Spending their days in total darkness, their eyes eventually atrophy. When brought up into the light they are found to be blind. The fish in Mammoth Cave, living for generations in total darkness, have no eyes! Ellen White has warned us on this point: "The spirit of hatred which has existed with some . . . has brought blindness and a fearful deception upon their own souls, making it impossible for them to discriminate between right and wrong. They have put out their own spiritual eyesight."—*Testimonies*, Vol. 3, p. 266. But "if we are constantly looking unto Jesus and receiving His Spirit, we shall have clear eyesight. Then we shall discern the perils on every side."—*Selected Messages*, Book Two, p. 60.

The Bible uses the eye to picture knowing. "I see it!" one may

EYE—DISCERNMENT OF GOD

exclaim today, and mean, "I now know!" or, "I perceive!" or, "I understand!" Solomon observed that "the eyes of the Lord preserve knowledge." (Proverbs 22:12.) The Spirit who comes from the councils of Deity has the special office of maintaining, among the faithful followers of Christ, the true knowledge of eternal things. Where His teaching ministry does not function, people remain ignorant of eternal realities. He who surrenders his will to the control of the Spirit Christ represents as plucking out his own eye, and giving over his view of life to the clearer and fuller views granted by the Spirit.

The eye betokens the freedom of personal judgment. Korah, Dathan, and Abiram felt that they had been gravely insulted in not being elected to the priesthood. When they spread their criticism of Moses among the people, the leader of Israel remonstrated with them. He pointed out that the decision as to who should be priests was exclusively the Lord's. He invited the rebels to come and talk over their grievances. Their reply was rude and arrogant, "We will not come up." Then they asked slyly, "Wilt thou put out the eyes of these men?" (Numbers 16:12, 14.) What they meant was, "Will your arguments so brainwash those who are opposing you that they will be unable to look at these things in their own way?" The renegades claimed freedom to view the issue as they chose. Eyes are used in this context as figurative of an individual point of view. With this in mind, the Hebrew law takes on a clearer meaning, "a gift [or bribe] doth blind the eyes of the wise." (Deuteronomy 16:19.) However, the eye of God impartially and clearly judges. Because of this the Spirit will give clear insights to His people and reveal their duties and responsibilities.

We use our eyes constantly to make decisions. We judge distances between two objects and the contrasts between two colors. We compute the height and length of what we see and estimate the numbers involved. The Scriptures often attribute these activities of Deity to His "eyes." Heaven scrutinizes the characters of men. "Noah found grace in the eyes of the Lord." Genesis 6:8. David "did that which was right in the eyes of the Lord." (1 Kings 15:5.) When the king proposed to restore the ark to its rightful place, he hoped that his act would "find favour in the eyes of the Lord." (2 Samuel 15:25.) By contrast the wicked deed of Onan "was evil in the eyes of the Lord" (Genesis 38:10, margin), as were David's sins (2 Samuel 11:27, Hebrew).

The prophet Amos warns us that the eyes of the Lord critically regard sinful persons, and that nothing escapes His searching gaze. (Amos 9:8.) Ezekiel notes that the Lord's eye does not spare the obdurate. (Ezekiel 5:11.) In contrast with this the Lord looks upon His people as "the apple of his eye." (Zechariah 2:8.) The Spirit is Heaven's Agent to carry out all these functions. His ministry is to convince of sin and warn of judgment. To do this, He must first see clearly. He easily detected the secret scheming of Ananias and Sapphira. God's eyes "try" (Psalm 11:4) the affairs of all men. He tests their motives carefully. Our prayer should be: "Eternal Spirit, criticize my actions and motives. 'Search me, O God, and know my heart: try me, and know my thoughts: and see if there be any wicked way in me, and lead me in the way everlasting.' Psalm 139:23, 24. Then, O Lord, give me grace and power to overcome, before it is forever too late." Jesus has promised that His Spirit will do just this for every trusting soul.

The Spirit acts as Judge. On several occasions when Israel apostatized, the eyes of the Lord noted their sins. (1 Kings 11:33; 14:8; 2 Kings 10:30.) As the Spirit seeks to keep the final judgment vividly before men, He anticipates the time when God will eventually have to hide His eyes from the wicked. This means that He has withdrawn His pleading Spirit from them. (Isaiah 1:15.) They will then be forever lost. The Spirit is the last contact of the soul with heaven. When the Spirit leaves the human heart, that person is doomed.

Christ used the eye as a symbol of perception. After He had

healed the man born blind, a discussion ensued between Him and the Pharisees. He had previously told them that even though they had eyes, they refused to see. (Mark 8:18.) Now He added, "If ye were blind, ye should have no sin: but now ye say, We see; therefore your sin remaineth." John 9:41. The Spirit alone can give clear perceptions of the true values of life to the human mind. Without the help of His discerning power, man dwells in the dark, for "he that lacketh these things is blind, and cannot see afar off." (2 Peter 1:9.) The Apostle Peter's word rendered *blind* is the root for myopia, shortsightedness, and underlines the idea that he who is without the Holy Ghost can but have limited views of life. He sees only his immediate surroundings. Yet while the human "eye hath not seen . . . the things which God hath prepared for them that love him, . . . God [has] revealed them unto us by his Spirit." (1 Corinthians 2:9, 10.) He is God's Agent to give divine perception to the devout Christian. When filled with the Holy Ghost, man's earthly view of life makes place for the heavenly vision. The Spirit will always be eyes for the disciple, whose grasp of the will of God will then be clear and constant.

The eye is one of our major safety factors. Good, clear eyesight enables us to avoid a thousand traps which would cause us to fall and hurt ourselves. Have you watched the fumbling care with which a blind man approaches the unknown? God has provided His children with celestial eyesight, too, as a defense against lurking spiritual dangers. The gospel prophet describes the amazing contributions which our Saviour made to redeem us. There was no human volunteer for this rescue operation, so Jesus gave Himself. (Isaiah 59:16-21.) Armed with grace for His desperate task, He fought the devil, suffered, died, and rose again victorious. In this recital of conflict and triumph, the divine assurance is given, "When the enemy shall come in like a flood, the Spirit of the Lord shall lift up a standard against him." Verse 19. Protection and victory come to the beleaguered saint through the silent and invisible but continual ministry of the Holy Spirit.

An interesting illustration of this is found in the narrative of the sacrifice of Isaac. When the ordeal was over, and Abraham had offered the lamb, caught in a thicket, in place of his son, he exultingly adored his God. The altar which he erected he named "Jehovah-jireh." (Genesis 22:14.) "Jireh" comes from the verb *to see,* which also has the idea of observing a need. The title may be rendered "God sees and provides." (Genesis 22:14, margin.) Today the observant Spirit notes our every requirement and proffers us the help we should have.

A blind man sways uncertainly as he gropes along an unknown way. His outstretched arms feel for handholds or obstacles. He uses a white stick to warn and guide. He does not know the lurking dangers. How often we have observed a kindly stranger take him by his arm and help him across a busy intersection. To some extent we all are spiritually blind and cannot always discern the road we should travel. We fumble uncertainly on our way to heaven, and yet the Holy Spirit stands ready to be eyes for us. He takes our stuttered prayers and makes them eloquent before God. (Romans 8:26.) He interprets our unspoken desires and focuses them. He grasps our fumbling, outstretched hands that seek for a sure waymark and guides them to God and a safe haven. All we have to do is to feel after heavenly things with all our desires, and the Spirit will help us to find them. He will enable us to keep our balance and equilibrium.

In the vision of the glory of God granted to Ezekiel, a conspicuous symbol was made up of wheels within wheels which were "full of eyes." (Ezekiel 1:16, 18; 10:12.) Ellen White interprets these involved pictures as the "complicated play of human events." The prophet further observed that these wheels were under the control of the Spirit. (Ezekiel 1:12, 20.) "So the complicated play of human events is under divine control. Amidst the strife and tumult of nations, He that sitteth above the cheru-

EYE—DISCERNMENT OF GOD

bim still guides the affairs of the earth."—*Education*, p. 178.

The Spirit sees all things in clearest perspective, He is never taken by surprise. The Spirit has His helpers, called the cherubim. The Revelator noted that they, too, were "full of eyes." (Revelation 4:6, 8.) Nothing is hidden from the eyes of Him with whom we have to do. When we submit ourselves and our affairs to the guidance of the all-seeing Spirit, we have nothing to fear. There is no emergency with God. He never slumbers or sleeps.

When the Beloved woos His bride, the church, "his eyes are as the eyes of doves." (Song of Solomon 5:12.) The dove, as we have noted, is a well-known emblem of the Spirit. (See chapter one.) Tender and loving, gentle and compassionate, the Holy Ghost is the Friend of the Bridegroom. His function is to propose to the bride on the Bridegroom's behalf. The joy in the eyes of his God will be reflected in the surrendered believer's heart. (Song of Solomon 4:9.)

But to those who finally spurn all appeals of the Spirit the end is tragic. The returning Bridegroom terrorizes them. The eyes of the Lord will then appear as "a flame of fire." (Revelation 1:14.) Searing, piercing, purging, destroying, revealing, nothing sinful will withstand their terrifying gaze!

Today the illuminating Spirit is willing to give us the vision we need. He will lift our vision from the sordid things of earth and open our minds to perceive the inner courts of heaven. He will reveal to us the machinations and designs of Satan, and vividly present the realities of spiritual things. With eyes sharpened by His presence, the sincere believer will even become aware of wickedness creeping into the church and thus be enabled to discern truth from error. We need little beyond this discernment of the Spirit to view and appropriate all the resources Christ has for our victory.

17.

VOICE --
Remembrancer of God

The tribes of Israel were ranged around the skirts of Sinai. When preparations for the encounter with Jehovah had been completed, God summoned Moses into the cloud-shrouded mountain. As a result "mount Sinai was altogether on a smoke, because the Lord descended upon it in fire: and the smoke thereof ascended as the smoke of a furnace, and the whole mount quaked greatly. And when the voice of the trumpet sounded long, and waxed louder and louder, Moses spake, and God answered him by a voice." (Exodus 19:18, 19.) The message which the Voice proclaimed that day was framed as law. (Exodus 20:1-17.) Today the Holy Spirit is God's Remembrancer of the ideals of love codified as law. What God's voice declared in thunder tones at Sinai, the Spirit quietly, daily teaches the disciple of Christ.

The Scriptures are God's Word. As we peruse them prayerfully, we shall hear His divine voice speaking to us personally. What we read is a "thus saith the Lord." Let us always carefully consider the words and spirit of Deity's communication to us. The Spirit is God's spokesman, and, through the Scriptures, Heaven's Remembrancer brings back to us the very words our Saviour spoke.

Long ago the patriarch of Uz remarked, "God speaketh once, yea twice, yet man perceiveth it not." Job 33:14. What are these two avenues along which Jehovah communicates with His children? He first spoke to man through His perfectly created works. God next talked to him through His personal word—the inspired Scriptures, and the incarnate Son. (Hebrews 1:1, 2.) But the "voice" of all creation is actually voiceless! "There is no speech nor language; their voice cannot be heard," the psalmist noted. (Psalm 19:1-3, R.V.) While heaven and earth still declare God's glory, this is largely incommunicable to us because we lack perception. Hence, in His compassion God speaks "twice." This second voice is the Holy Spirit, who unfolds to us the meaning of creation and gives us an understanding of God's will for our lives. Yet in spite of all this "man perceiveth not." The sinner's "heart is waxed gross, and [his] ears are dull of hearing." (Matthew 13:15.) But then Jesus came to open the ears of the deaf. Now His Spirit enables us to hear. He is God's Remembrancer of the words of both creation and redemption.

God's voice talks to us through the dictates of our consciences. When educated and regulated by the divine law of love, this faculty approves the good and condemns the bad. To the Christian who honestly responds to this censor, rebuilt by God's grace, the Spirit provides both check and countercheck in all life's decisions. By His ministry the trusting soul discovers that "the path of the just is as the shining light, that shineth more and more unto the perfect day." (Proverbs 4:18.) The Spirit is God's Remembrancer of the road the pilgrim must travel to the Promised Land.

The voice of the Spirit is more than a message or an inspired record in an inspired book. Voice presupposes the presence of a person speaking living words. It tells of proximity and conveys personality in tones of love in rebuke, appeal, or encouragement. The voice is intimate and warm as "the sound of a gentle stillness [or "whisper"]." (1 Kings 19:12, margin.) All these qualities the Spirit conveys. He whispers to our hearts, and we recognize the Good Shepherd calling His sheep.

The speaking of her name, "Mary!" brought the weeping girl joyously to Jesus' feet. His voice revealed the presence of her Lord. His voice had stilled the fears of children and the raging of the storm. The voice of the Spirit speaks today in the tones of the affectionate Father and His gracious Son. The Holy Spirit is God's Remembrancer of our fellowship in the heavenly family.

But in what ways does the Spirit actually speak to us? He explains the vocabulary of the truth. He does this, first, through the Scriptures. These sacred books He Himself caused to be written and preserved. In them we hear His voice telling us of divine wisdom and mercy, love and justice. He takes the very words and passages we read in God's Book, the events and incidents there described, and irradiates them with heavenly light so that they appear relevant in time and application to our experiences.

Christ is the Word of God, Heaven's final communication to man. (Hebrews 1:1, 2.) "See that ye refuse not him that speaketh," Paul warns us. (Hebrews 12:25.) The message He brings to our hearts may not necessarily reveal what is new. It may not lead us into unknown territory, for God has already given man all he needs to know regarding the way of salvation. But His Spirit's message is always pertinent and vital. The Holy Ghost is God's Remembrancer of the precise truths we each need to know day by day.

The Scriptures contain the full and unalterable revelation regarding the divine plan for vindicating God's character and helping repentant sinners to Paradise. These truths have come to man by special unfoldings of knowledge brought about through the Spirit's employment of certain "holy" men as His agents. The unaided human mind could never have perceived these insights. (1 Corinthians 2:9-12.)

Nowadays the Spirit employs the Word He has already inspired, caused to be written out, and miraculously preserved through the centuries, as His agency in awakening the unwary sinner. The incorruptible "Word of God" produces in the penitent perceptions of Christ and engenders a desire for renewal. To accomplish this, the Lord most frequently employs "the foolishness of preaching" accompanied by a "demonstration of the Spirit and *[viz.]* of power." (1 Corinthians 1:21; 2:4.) As we carefully and prayerfully read the inspired Scriptures, we may distinctly hear the voice of God calling as "deep calleth unto deep" (Psalm 42:7) and awakening our interest and illuminating our minds. The Spirit is still God's Remembrancer through the oracles He inspired long ago.

God's voice may also speak to the inmost soul and cause the inmost ear to hear, producing a restless and uneasy mind. The conscience will then awaken, either to sense sin or to a longing for righteousness. Our conscience may continue to disturb us, but it sends these alarms in kindness. Impressions of new points of view should be carefully compared with the Scriptures. When the two—our ideas of what we ought to do and what the Bible says—agree, we may be sure that the Spirit's voice is directing our lives.

Have you heard the voice of God in your soul as you read the Scriptures? Have you felt some foreboding of unknown danger or consciousness of past sin and condemnation of your present conduct? Have you sensed an urging toward specific reformation or a desire awakened for revival? Have you not read on and grown vividly aware of the voice speaking to you? Has He called your attention to this or that Bible character as a mirror of your life? Someone who did a wrong in days of old that you must studiously avoid! Or perhaps, what another character did you must emulate. The Spirit assures you that his source of strength may also be yours. His temptations parallel your own. Do you realize who it is that thus excites your thoughts? Do you understand who urges you on to a better way of life? Ask yourself, Can these inner dynamics result from my own carnal mind alone? You will agree with my answer. No! They are the suggestions of the good Spirit drawing you into conversation with Himself. Your sinful motives He seeks to purify. You have strayed. He would bring you back to the path of righteousness. An unknown poet thus succinctly summarizes what I have been trying to say:

> "Oh, sinner! 'twas a heavenly voice,
> It was the Spirit's gracious call;
> It bade you make the better choice,
> And haste to seek in Christ your all."
> —*Anonymous.*

Does your heart bear witness that these are the actual results when you truly study the Bible with prayer and a sincere desire to find out your Lord's will? Is this your Christian experience with the things of your inner life when you really worship? How carefully then should we consider the Spirit's wooings! How studiously should we seek to understand! How diligently should we obey! How often should we slip away from the din of life to the quiet of an audience with the Divine and, through His Word, listen to the still small voice of the Spirit speaking in our souls.

Have you ever looked into your mind and wondered why one idea followed another? External objects begin a train of thought. Ideas awaken and very soon chase one another across the fields of your mind, pausing a moment at one point, and then darting to another apparently unrelated to it. Some have labeled this process "the law of association." One thought suggests another quite closely related to it. This in turn suggests a third, and so on until the fiftieth idea is not even remotely akin to the original one! This kind of vague thinking is almost useless! The Christian must bring his thoughts into captivity to God's will. His purpose should be directed to the throwing down of "imaginations, and every high thing that exalteth itself against the knowledge of God." (2 Corinthians 10:5.) You can accomplish this kind of thought control by deliberately fixing your mind on some object. Then carefully edit, sift, and discipline the ideas which flow into the formation of trains of thought, like cars attached to a railroad engine. "The mind enlightened by the Holy Spirit may discern that it is diverging from the right way."—*Testimonies*, Vol. 8, pp. 290, 291. God's voice is the Remembrancer of right thinking.

While God speaks to us through His Word, He also communicates through the providential experiences of our lives. The Spirit uses these to direct our thoughts toward eternal realities. He associates celestial objectives with terrestrial ideas. If we consciously submit our lives to the keeping of His Spirit, as we deliberately pray that our wills shall be subordinated to His, the Spirit will overrule external stimuli upon our thoughts. What might have been a temptation to turn the channel of our thinking unto unworthy lines, He will make a vehicle to suggest loftier ideals. A Scripture passage, some incident in our daily lives, even an inanimate object about us, the Spirit will use to lead our minds into the contemplation of the ideal dynamics of conduct. These thoughts in the surrendered Christian may at first seem natural and no different from a thousand other thought trains of other days and circumstances, but an overruling Providence will soon be discovered to be actually controlling them. The Spirit will direct our lives into patterns of usefulness to our fellows, adoration of God, and our own well-being and happiness in this life and the next. This kind of Spirit-controlled meditation will ultimately have the most important bearing on our course of conduct. The Holy Spirit is God's Remembrancer of heavenly thinking.

Jesus promised that when the Spirit came from the Father at His prayer, He would "*convince* the world of sin, . . . because they believe not on me." (John 16:8, 9, margin.) The sin of unbelief is "the sin which doth so easily beset us." (Hebrews 12:1.) The Spirit awakens the dormant conscience through the ministry of law, for "by the law is the knowledge of sin." (Romans 3:20.) This was true of Paul, for he affirmed, "I had not known sin, but by the law." Romans 7:7. What, then, is the sin of unbelief? It is the rejection of the Spirit as the supreme Power in our lives. He presents Christ as the ever-loving, compassionate Redeemer and offers us the free gift of eternal life. Unbelief is contempt of His authority, rejection of His love. It is tantamount to calling God a liar and His plan for reconciliation a myth. It is regarding "the blood of the covenant . . . an unholy thing." Unbelief serves as the womb of all sins. The Holy Spirit, through the Scriptures, presents us with a portrayal of what God would do for us and the consequences of rejecting it. Besides this, He convicts us of our sin. The voice of the Spirit then convinces us of righteousness. He is God's Remembrancer of right and wrong.

The Spirit shows the path of virtue which leads to glory. His voice appeals to our hearts. To still this voice means to remain in sin. To receive His testimony is to believe all that the Word reveals. To accept His guidance is to distrust self and "have faith in God" alone, relying upon His promises. The voice of the Spirit calls upon us to believe the truth completely—"all truth"—and not merely a part. And Jesus is truth! The Spirit is God's Remembrancer of our Saviour and Lord.

The Holy Spirit also "will *convince* . . . of righteousness." (John 16:8, margin, 10.) We discover from the Scriptures that "all thy commandments are righteousness." (Psalm 119:172.) Of Christ it is said, He "is made unto us . . . righteousness." (1 Corinthians 1:30.) Our Saviour perfectly lived out all the principles of right conduct and then died for our sins. He was resurrected to grant us "the righteousness of God which is by faith of Jesus Christ unto all and upon all them that believe." (Romans 3:22.) Notice it is given *unto* and *upon* us. It reaches all the way. He imputes His righteousness to each of us, when we believe. But we must accept the gift He presents. By this act our faith is revealed. In this transaction God manifests His justice as He covers us "with the robe of righteousness." (Isaiah 61:10.)

VOICE—REMEMBRANCER OF GOD

The function of the voice of the Spirit is "to declare, I say, at this time his righteousness: that he might be just, and the justifier of him which believeth in Jesus." (Romans 3:26.) How careful should we be that when His voice says, "Today!" we shall not harden our hearts as Israel did in the long ago. The Spirit's voice is the wooing call of Heaven. He is God's Remembrancer that the Bridegroom awaits the return of His bride.

The Spirit's voice convinces of *righteousness,* for Jesus explained that this was "because I go to my Father." (John 16:10.) Our Lord's Spokesman constantly reminds us that while on earth Jesus lived and died for us. Now, once more united with the Father, "he ever liveth to make intercession" for us. (Hebrews 7:25.) Because He went to His Father's presence and there intercedes on our behalf, He will one day "appear the second time without sin unto salvation" to gather us to the Father's home. (Hebrews 9:28.) The Holy Spirit's voice constitutes Heaven's assurance of the reality of Christ's ministry. He is God's Remembrancer that the advent is not far distant.

The process of justification must affect each believer individually. Each disciple must personally be born from above and develop his Christian life. Unfortunately, however, each follower of Jesus does not grow in grace and knowledge at the same rate, nor does he attain to the same degree of sanctification. Some may remain as "newborn babes" far too long. Others stay as "little children" when they should be developing into Christian maturity. Some reach a state in which they "are of full age." Let each of us carefully examine his own heart to discover his true state.

It is the voice of the Spirit that convinces of *judgment.* (John 16:8, 11.) This function presents the judicial standard of excellence we must attain. The Spirit warns of what is wrong (sin) and of what is right (righteousness) and ever holds before our gaze the norm by which we should daily compare ourselves and by which God will eventually judge us. This standard is "the uplifting calling of God in Christ" (Philippians 3:14, Greek), which tugs us continually toward the ideal of "a perfect man." This goal is possible in "the fulness of Christ" (Ephesians 4:13) and by His free grace only. The voice of the Spirit is God's Remembrancer inviting us to look to Jesus only and grow like Him.

Prophecy presents the picture of God's method of calling the attention of mankind to His final saving message. John sees three angels speeding from race to race and from tribe to tribe. (Revelation 14:6-12.) Each has his special evangel. This he proclaims so as to be heard by all. (Verse 7.) In commenting upon the ultimatum presented by the third angel, Ellen White declares: "This message embraces the two preceding messages. It is represented as being given with a loud voice; that is, with the power of the Holy Spirit. Everything is now at stake. The third angel's message is to be regarded as of the highest importance. It is a life and death question. The impression made by this message will be proportionate to the earnestness and solemnity with which it is proclaimed."—*Seventh-day Adventist Bible Commentary,* Vol. 7, p. 980. "Voice" in this prophecy is employed as an emblem of the Spirit. Its loudness represents His power to be heard around the world. The voice is God's Remembrancer that the end of all things is at hand.

We notice, again, that "voice" points to the dynamic of the Spirit. Consistently, through the Scriptures, Inspiration has called attention to the voice of God. In every age the Spirit has been the divine Spokesman. In the stillness, a whisper reaches the soul of the despondent individual alone in the desert with his discouragement. It also speaks in accents of thunder before the universe. The voice of God is His most personal means of communicating with us.

The voice mirrors the inner emotions. The voice of God reveals His paternal sentiments to us. To listen to the "voice of the Beloved," or Adored One, is to hear the Bridegroom tenderly calling to His betrothed. To hear His voice from Sinai is to listen to the proclamation of the Great Legislator lovingly setting before His subjects the principles of right and wrong. To catch the tones of finality in the declaration, "Depart from me," is to hear the eternal Judge regretfully passing His unchangeable sentence because the obdurate have spurned His love. When the Scriptures call upon us to "hear his voice," they appeal to us to obey. Our Saviour referred with satisfaction to this thought when He noted, "My sheep hear my voice." John 10:27. On Christ's behalf the Spirit pleads with mankind to enter the sheepfold. His voice is God's Remembrancer that danger dogs the steps of the unwary.

Let us reiterate, God created by His Spirit when He "spake, and it was done." (Psalm 33:9.) The Legislator presented His law through His Spirit when the voice proclaimed His will from Sinai. (Exodus 19:19.) The Comforter assured His troubled prophet of God's unchanging love by "a still small voice." (1 Kings 19:12.) He desires to reveal Himself to His servant in the same way today. This quiet voice has power to change the heart of man.

Man, however, must choose to place himself where he can listen to the voice of the Spirit. But many do not hasten to where they can listen to Christ through the Holy Spirit. Social and business activities drown out that quiet voice, and eternal realities fade. Some do not shoulder present responsibilities. When such Christians discern what they should do for their Master, they dismiss the thought immediately. Yet "the voice of duty is the voice of God—an inborn, heaven-sent guide—and the Lord will not be trifled with upon these subjects. He who disregards the light which God has given . . . revolts against his own good, and refuses to obey the One who is working for his best good."—Ellen G. White, *Counsels on Health,* p. 562; compare with *The Desire of Ages,* p. 213.

18.

SAP--
Life Current of God

Sap is the liquid found in stems and roots of plants. Botanists describe two kinds. One sort, made up of water containing dissolved minerals, moves upward through the tree from the roots to the leaves. Its path lies in the layer of the stem and trunk of plants called the xylem, just under the bark. How does this kind of sap come into being and work? Tiny hairlike roots absorb the mineral-bearing water in the soil by osmosis. From these minute hairs the sap moves up the roots, and once it touches the xylem, it travels up this layer to every part of the plant until it eventually reaches the leaves. This vital liquor provides the minerals for the growth of the plant.

When the sun warms the leaves, their water content evaporates. Ninety-five percent of the sap thus dissipates into the air. This process in turn draws more water up into the leaves from the roots and the stem. As the moisture in the stem diminishes, water is again drawn up through the plant from the roots. The heat of the sun perpetuates this process. This pull of the sap along the xylem always comes from above. In plants and young trees this layer, also called sapwood, embraces the entire plant. In older trees the sapwood lies immediately under the bark and

Sap—Life Current of God

penetrates only a short distance into the major part of the trunk, which in turn is called heartwood. The sapwood is of a different color, much paler, and also much softer and weaker than the heartwood. It succumbs easily to the attack of termites and wood borers of many kinds.

The leaves produce the other kind of sap observed by botanists. The cells of leaves have the ability to absorb carbon dioxide from the air. This gas mixes with about 2 percent of the sap already pervading the leaves and forms into carbohydrates by releasing into the atmosphere the oxygen in the carbon dioxide. These carbohydrates dissolved in the leaf water form the juice which travels from the leaves down through the stems and trunk to the very roots. This sap provides the food for the growth of the plant or tree.

In the maple, and some other trees, the sap which rises may also contain carbohydrates at certain times of the year. This sap is collected and evaporated to turn it into sugar.

An average apple tree lifts and distributes to every part of the plant and eventually evaporates into the atmosphere four gallons of sap water an hour. When we consider the millions of trees and plants which surround us, the enormous quantity of moisture passing into the atmosphere through these living things is staggering!

The first sort of sap described carries the essential minerals of the earth up into the plant. The second kind brings into the plant the food elements from above. Both earth and heaven, so to speak, provide the essentials for growth. The importance of this liquid to maintain all forms of life is obvious. Sap may be called the life current of nature.

Sap plays a vital role not only in maintaining the living cells, but also in helping the growth of new cells in all plants. When the flow stops, and the moisture no longer supplies the carbohydrates and minerals, the cells die, the plant ceases to grow, and the fibers eventually dry up. Bereft of this life-bringing tide which inhibits the encroachment of bugs, the wood becomes the prey of insects and fungi, and decay and disintegration result.

The life cycle of the sap constitutes a revealing parable of the ministry of the Holy Spirit in the experience of the disciple of Christ. Ellen G. White observed concerning Christ's parable: "The sap of the vine, ascending from the root, is diffused to the branches, sustaining growth and producing blossoms and fruit. So the life-giving power of the Holy Spirit, proceeding from the Saviour, pervades the soul, renews the motives and affections, and brings even the thoughts into obedience to the will of God, enabling the receiver to bear the precious fruit of holy deeds." —*The Acts of the Apostles*, p. 284. Let us carefully study the words which are used in these sentences.

Mrs. White's first observation calls attention to the sap "ascending from the root." The ministry of the Spirit is basic. We must be rooted in Him. Then His presence, bringing all the elements of spiritual growth into the life, will diffuse them to "the branches." No part of the Christian's life can exist independently of Him, for He alone sustains growth and produces blossoms and fruit.

Ellen White further observed, "Abiding in Christ means a constant receiving of His Spirit, a life of unreserved surrender to His service. The channel of communication must be open continually between man and his God. As the vine branch constantly draws the sap from the living vine, so are we to cling to Jesus."—*The Desire of Ages*, p. 676. The sap constantly works in the living plants. In the same way the Christian must allow the Spirit continual dominance in his life, receiving from Him only heavenly influences.

The sap is invisible and constantly at work in every fiber of the plant. "The communication of life, strength, and fruitfulness from the root to the branches is unobstructed and constant. Separated from the vine, the branch cannot live. No more, said Jesus, can you live apart from Me. The life you have received from Me

Sap—Life Current of God

can be preserved only by continual communion. Without Me you cannot overcome one sin, or resist one temptation."—*Ibid.*, p. 676. Like the sap, the presence of the Spirit in the heart is hidden from view. The evidence that the living current is actually flowing through us is that we bear healthy fruit. Like this nurturing fluid, the Spirit makes no outward show of His presence. He is interested only in the final results. His power enables the Christian life to reach its goal in abundant fruit bearing.

The sap provides all the life-forces for the perfect development of the plant. It works from the inside, and its effectiveness is later witnessed by foliage and fruitfulness. In the same way the Spirit must renew the motives and affections of the Christian's inner being. When the sap ceases to flow, the dynamic of vigorous growth is no more at work. How often the Christian becomes sadly conscious that he is no longer as strongly motivated as he used to be when he started out on his discipleship. His views of his Lord have grown dim, his affection for Christ and His kingdom has waned and may even be displaced by other loves. He ceases to be Christ-centered. Yet the Spirit is ready to keep the thoughts and motives, the affections and impulses, turned toward righteousness, bright and warm. Like the sap in plants, the Spirit preserves the vitality of the Christian's drive toward God.

The sap pervades the living plant. No part of it can live without this life-bringing presence. This is also true of the Holy Spirit. His abiding presence vitalizes every detail, every aspect of the disciple's life. His holy power must sanctify every aspiration and activity. For our discipleship to be dynamic and growing with the Spirit within, we can hold no secret corner of our lives away from Him, no cherished loves, no surreptitious grip on things of time and sense. Our roving thoughts must be displaced with Spirit-inspired ideals and then consciously fixed on things of eternity.

The flow of the sap is generated from above. The power of the sun draws the vital moisture up from the roots. Bearing its life-sustaining elements, it irrigates the cells of the entire plant with nourishment. This fact finds its parallel in the experience of every saint. At the summons of the Sun of Righteousness, the Spirit flows through the Christian with life-giving power. Not only does He nurture every phase of the individual life; He also supports each branch, every member of the body of Christ, in his growth and witness. Christ's omnipotent power directs the Spirit-filled life. We do not use the Spirit; He uses us. The branch does not supply the sap. The sap enables the limb to become a branch in the first place and then helps it grow and fulfill its destiny in life—to bring forth much fruit—to stretch out into another life, or multitudes of lives. Ellen White penetratingly observes, "All created beings live by the will and power of God. They are dependent recipients of the life of God. From the highest seraph to the humblest animate being, all are replenished from the Source of life."—*The Desire of Ages*, p. 785. The Spirit is the life essence of God in the surrendered soul.

Our attention is called to the fact that "the root sends it nourishment through the branch to the outermost twig. So Christ communicates the current of spiritual strength to every believer. So long as the soul is united to Christ, there is no danger that it will wither or decay."—*Ibid.*, p. 676. Each branch participates in the same life-giving power. There is no disharmony between limb and limb. All are united in building up because they participate in the same spiritual essence. Each brings forth the same fruit, which is essentially love in its many-hued splendor. While some branches may mutate and produce better and more vigorous growth and more luscious fruit, basically all branches have the same nature. We should pray that the Spirit flowing through us will give us Heaven's unity in earth's diversity.

Sap flows silently and imperceptibly in the plant. It climbs the inner fibers of the tree with no martial tread or peal of trumpet. Likewise, in quietness, the Spirit works in the life. Like the sap rising in the plant, His ministry is not perceptible hour by

Sap—Life Current of God

hour or day by day. But when the season for life's harvest comes round, the "peaceable fruit of righteousness," ripe and beautiful, will appear on the branches. Fruit testifies that the divine Essence has filled the life. The noisy, the exciting, and the ecstatic are not necessary. God would have us heed His admonition. "Be still, and know that I am God." Psalm 46:10. We should remember that the process is not as important as the result. Our prayer should be, "Eternal Spirit, work constantly in us to bring forth. Thy fruit in righteousness."

The branch possesses the same life and nature as the trunk and root. By this organic union there results a vital relationship, "the life of the vine becomes the life of the branch. So the soul dead in trespasses and sins receives life through connection with Christ. By faith in Him as a personal Saviour the union is formed. The sinner unites his weakness to Christ's strength, his emptiness to Christ's fullness, his frailty to Christ's enduring might. Then he has the mind of Christ. The humanity of Christ has touched our humanity, and our humanity has touched divinity. Thus through the agency of the Holy Spirit man becomes a partaker of the divine nature. He is accepted in the Beloved."—*Ibid.*, p. 675. The Holy Spirit brings into the very fibers of our humanity the divine nature of Jesus, our Elder Brother. We thus become bone of His bone and flesh of His flesh. He shares His life of triumph with us, and we participate in His power daily to develop into His likeness and bring forth fruit pleasing to the Husbandman. The Holy Spirit brings this heavenly sap, this essential life current of the divine nature into our being.

Sap contains all the food elements necessary to maintain life and cause further growth in the plant. Look at the beautiful jacaranda tree in bloom, its limbs garlanded with blossoms! Have you ever wondered how the fibers of the roots pluck from the soil the ingredients which make the bark brown, the leaves green, the blooms blue, and the heartwood black? Have you tried to picture the substances which add gold dust to the stamens and the gentle perfume to the flowers? The heartwood is hard and tough, the blossoms soft and fragile, while the bark is friable and brittle. The river of life which flows up from the roots and meets the stream cascading from the leaves provides every element needed for the perfect development of every part of the tree, whether we understand how or not.

In like manner the Spirit bestows upon us the stream of living grace for our Christian development. The soft, warm affections which bind brother to brother in Christlike love spring from the Holy Ghost. The Spirit also sustains those masculine virtues of firmness in standing for the right, and demonstrating the vitality which affirms, "though he slay me, yet will I trust in him." The fragrance of Christian meekness and the fertilizing energy which bring forth fruit also owe their origin and continued force to the life current of God. Since we are so dependent upon the Spirit, with what insistence should we implore His presence in our lives!

The elements present in the soil in which the roots grow dramatically affect the mineral content of the sap. If some of the salts upon which the plant depends have been leeched out of the soil, the roots will not find them. This lack will reveal itself not only in inadequate growth of plant or tree, but also in the poor quality of foliage and fruit. Have you considered the specific elements of godly living which the Spirit provides for each of us? The attitude which esteems our brother better than ourselves produces meekness, humility, and respect, and banishes politics and discrimination. The ideal of dedication to God makes us faithful Christians, vigilant watchmen, and sacrificial shepherds. Service to our fellows and witnessing to our faith naturally spring up when the Spirit abides in our hearts.

The quality of the sap affects the defense mechanism of orchard trees. A perfectly healthy plant more strongly resists viral and fungal pests than one lacking the vital elements. This point clearly applies to "the trees of righteousness," which represent Christians. Without the daily filling and flowing of the life cur-

Sap—Life Current of God

rent of the Spirit in his life, the disciple is at the mercy of every corrosive enterprise of Satan to degenerate his thoughts, to poison his purposes, and to fasten upon him every species of evil habit. How often has an evangelist observed that when the transforming power of the Spirit changes the current of life in a new convert, all the wrong habits of decades drop off. When the divine Essence sets the heart right, the outward deportment will become right, too. The inner sap of the Spirit guarantees that the degenerative forces of Satan shall be neutralized, and good fruit borne.

There are definite seasons during which sap rises in full flood. After the sleep of the cold winter months, the dormant plants and trees respond to the genial call of the sun. Even before the freezing weather completely passes, while the snow still lies in drifts about the trees, the mechanism for the flowing of the sap is triggered. The invisible sun issues his orders, and all nature springs into action. The tiny hairlike fibers begin to drink deep drafts of water, and all vegetation surges with life. God has left us His promise of a definite time for the full flowing of the Spirit into our lives. When the night of sin has almost gone, when the lethargic sleep of the church has run its course, then the "Sun of righteousness [will rise] with healing in his wings," and at His bidding the Spirit will start the new momentum in the Christian's life. New growth in preparation for new fruit will result. Earth's harvest time is not far off. The ground has been prepared. The seed has been sown, and the heavenly Husbandman awaits the peaceable fruit of righteousness. He has promised to send out the call for the nurturing Spirit's ministry at the right time. The heavenly sap will supply the elements for perfect growth and fullest fruit bearing. The spring and harvest, the early and latter rain, the birth and the maturity—each requires the work of the Spirit. The Spirit is prepared to fulfill His ministry. Unlike the plants, we Christians have the choice ever before us. When we ask, the Lord will give without a grudging hand.

The quantity and quality of the sap depend upon the

moisture content of the soil. If this is arid, there can be no sap, and shrubs and trees wither and die. But when the rain comes and the earth is once more moist, the sap starts flowing freely. Everything which grows in the soil drinks deeply and again lives a full and normal life. God has promised that He will send the rain, the early and the latter rain, seedtime and harvest rain, birth-bringing and fruit-producing rain, to cause the inner sap of our discipleship to surge. The Spirit without, the Spirit within, are the same Spirit working toward the same end, the fullness of the Christian's life in God.

Even Christ's "life was constantly sustained by fresh inspirations of the Holy Spirit." (*Testimonies*, Vol. 5, p. 161.) How much more necessary that we ensure that our supply of the life current of God is never stopped or deflected from our daily experiences. We should ever pray: "Sap of the heavenly Vine, constantly give Thy life to me."

EPILOGUE

Now we have come to the end of our study of the Holy Spirit, viewed through the windows He Himself has opened into His ministry. We have observed His concern for us as Christ's family. We have noted His gentleness as well as His mighty power. We have walked in the light of His eye and followed the direction His finger has pointed. We have experienced the warmth of His breath and listened to the soft cadences of His voice.

For us the light of a new day has dawned, and we have noted the things of God washed fresh with rain. The plants of the heavenly Gardener are garlanded with dew and flowing with sap. The wind has cleared the atmosphere, and the light of Heaven streams into the secret recesses of our lives.

Within our hearts His fire burns with affectionate regard, because as Christ's bride we have the comforting assurance of an everlasting dowry. He seals our hearts and places the perfume of Paradise upon our heads. The fare of God is ever spread before us, salted with the flavor of His salt. And from the trees in God's garden the Dove of Heaven calls to us as we walk to the tree of life in the soft luminance of His presence.

The presence of the Spirit brings the person of Christ within our comprehension and reach. Our Saviour could have given us no greater boon than to give us His Spirit. How much we should love the Giver and His Gift and, in appreciation of what the Giver has done and ever does for us, value His Gift and His limitless ministry.

Eternal Spirit, we love Thee for Thyself and also for making our blessed Jesus so much more precious.

We'd love to have you download our catalog of
titles we publish at:

www.TEACHServices.com

or write or email us your thoughts,
reactions, or criticism about this
or any other book we publish at:

TEACH Services, Inc.
254 Donovan Road
Brushton, NY 12916

info@TEACHServices.com

or you may call us at:

518/358-3494

Produced in partnership with
LNFBooks.com

www.ingramcontent.com/pod-product-compliance
Lightning Source LLC
Chambersburg PA
CBHW072030170426
43200CB00025B/2449